THE MORNING THE SUN WENT DOWN

THE MORNING THE SUN WENT DOWN

Darryl Babe Wilson

Foreword by Malcolm Margolin

HEYDAY
Berkeley, California

The publisher thanks Beatrice Bowles, Gregg Castro, Sandy Cold Shapero, Linda and John Hussa, Dorothy Martinez, Marion Weber, and RB9 Publishing for their generous contributions to this project.

Second edition 2016
© 1998, 2016 by Darryl Babe Wilson
Foreword © 2016 by Malcolm Margolin

Library of Congress Cataloging-in-Publication Data
Names: Wilson, Darryl Babe, 1939-2014, author.
Title: The morning the sun went down / Darryl Babe Wilson.
Description: Berkeley, California : Heyday, [2016] | First published:
  Berkeley, California : Heyday Books, 1998.
Identifiers: LCCN 2016019133 | ISBN 9781597143622 (paperback : alkaline paper)
Subjects: LCSH: Wilson, Darryl Babe, 1939-2014—Childhood and youth. |
  Achomawi Indians—Biography. | Atsugewi Indians—Biography. | Pit River
  Tribe, California—Biography. | Achomawi Indians—Social life and customs.
  | Atsugewi Indians—Social life and customs. | Indian foster
  children—California—Biography. | Indians of North America—Cultural
  assimilation—California—History—20th century. | Off-reservation
  boarding schools—California—History—20th century. | California—Race
  relations—History—20th century.
Classification: LCC E99.A15 W55 2016 | DDC 979.4004/97—DC23
LC record available at https://lccn.loc.gov/2016019133

Cover Design: Ashley Ingram
Cover Photograph: John Westrock
Interior Design/Typesetting: Thomas Christensen

Orders, inquiries, and correspondence should be addressed to:
  Heyday
  P. O. Box 9145, Berkeley, CA 94709
  (510) 549-3564, Fax (510) 549-1889
  www.heydaybooks.com

Printed in East Peoria, IL, by Versa Press, Inc.

10 9 8 7 6 5 4 3 2 1

FSC
www.fsc.org
MIX
Paper from
responsible sources
FSC® C005010

to all my children

CONTENTS

ACKNOWLEDGMENTS

Immediately after graduating from the University of California at Davis in 1991, I accepted a full scholarship to the University of Arizona, Tucson, in pursuit of a Master of Arts degree through the American Indian Studies Program. At Tucson I was encouraged by the members of my Master of Arts committee to continue developing the Park field notes (narratives and other material that anthropologist Susan Park had gathered from my people in Hat Creek and Dixie Valley in 1931; see Glossary), with the idea of preparing them for publication as part of the requirements for my degree. Which I did by creating *Yokenaswi Yusji* (Necklace of Animal Hearts), a volume of narration that is pending publication at the University of Arizona.

Then I began earnestly working on this manuscript, in part because my committee insisted that the expressions of my people be catapulted out of the shadowy mists of mythology and into the lighted arena of literature.

As a consequence, there are many people who encouraged this little volume into existence. Some of you could not have known that your interest and genuine concern would appear in this form, nor could I, and some great people just have to be mentioned:

My seven sons, especially the twins Seterro (Hoss) and Theo (Boss), who began working with me on the Susan Park field notes while they were second graders at Davis. They have continued this writing/academic adventure with me (they are now entering their junior year in high school), Seterro, in the process, becoming a poet in his own right—which thrills me.

All of my tribal people, especially those Elders of Wisdom. They are the keepers of our narratives and knowledge revealing what we are privileged to know upon special occasions.

Those strong people in the Pit River/Hat Creek mountains who have supported my academic dreams are Hyram and Dorothy Brown of McArthur, California; Georgie Hess, XL Ranch, Alturas, California; LaVerna Jenkins and Lillian Snooks, Hat Creek, California; and both the Mike and the Buckskin families of Dana in the Pit River Country.

My academic foundation at the University of California, Davis, was provided by Drs. Jack Hicks, Gary Snyder, Jack Forbes, Steve Crum, Martha Macri, Inez Hernandez-Avila, David Risling Jr., Stefano Varese, John O. Stewart, and David Scofield Wilson. Secretary Jerry Kemp, the people at the Woman's Research Center, and Mr. Michael Harrison of the Harrison Western Research Center, Live Oak, California, are my guardian spirits.

At the University of Arizona, my academic support commission includes Drs. Ofelia Zepeda and Larry Evers (both members of my masters and doctoral committees), Tom Holm, Ellen Basso, Jane Hill (President of the American Anthropology Association), Michelle Grijalva, and Jay Stauss; while Dr. Adela A. Allen and Georgia Ehlers, are my administrative platform.

Upon the greater scaffold of humankind there is a network of organizations and individuals who have been of immense support and encouragement to me. The Ford Foundation adopted me as a fellow, supporting my academic pursuit as though I were running a race for an Olympic Gold Medal and their honor was subject to my performance.

There is Mike Williams (fellow student) of Davis who joined my black-tie-only-banquet on the 26th floor of the Gannett Building (where *USA Today* is published) in Arlington, Virginia. He wore Levi's, a T-shirt, and a leather jacket that appeared to have survived several uprisings! Also, there are Jerry and JoAnn Aronson (formerly of Fall River Mills) who kept the twins and me alive as we managed to somehow survive in the mountains with no means of support except woodcutting. Jerry bought our wood even though he did not need it, and watched while the twins, between their third and sixth year, became pretty good at splitting oak and stacking it.

I was tolerated and assisted immensely at the American Indian Graduate Center at the University of Arizona by the capable people working there: Glenn Johnson, Director, and the secretaries Donna Treloar and Leslie Durhman (who probably still want to choke me for remaining illiterate in computer technology).

And I would be shockingly remiss not to mention Jeannine Gendar, the editor of *News from Native California;* Kim Bancroft and Laura Harger, the editors of this manuscript; Malcolm Margolin, of both *News from Native California* and Heyday Books; Mary Bates Abbott of Advocates for the Survival of California Languages and Native California Network; Marion Weber from the Flow Fund; and Reitha B. (Tiny) Amen, a person of my tribe. Immediately after the lumber truck–automobile wreck described in this book, she cared for us surviving children. And she did something that all of the king's horses and all of the king's men could not do for Humpty Dumpty. She pieced all eight of our shattered spirits back together again.

I thank you each (and all you precious people, both in academia and in the general society, who are not mentioned here but most certainly should be), and someday, since I must keep trying, I may accomplish something that you all will be proud of.

—D.B.W.

FOREWORD
to the 2016 edition

Darryl Wilson was constantly on the move, driven from
one city to another, sometimes in response to opportunity,
sometimes pushed by need, sometimes seeking refuge from
yet another of the personal disasters that so remorselessly
pursued him throughout his life. When I first met him
in the late 1980s, he was living in Davis. His wife, Danell
Garcia, had died—tragically and ironically like his mother,
in an automobile accident—and he had only recently
pulled himself out of the depths of despair, enrolled at
UC Davis, and was struggling to get a bachelor's degree
while raising two infant sons, the twins Seterro and Theo
(known throughout Indian country as Hoss and Boss).
Then came the years he spent in Tucson, where he got
a Ph.D. at the University of Arizona; in San Jose, where
he was cobbling together a livelihood as a lecturer at a
number of colleges, traveling the state as a storyteller, and
turning out a body of literature—at once lyrical, angry,
and visionary—that would gain him friends and admir-
ers everywhere; and in Gardnerville, Nevada, where he

was teaching culture and language to young Washo tribal members. In 2000, while in Nevada, he suffered a nearly fatal stroke that left him severely disabled. He returned to San Jose, then moved to Santa Cruz, California, where he lived with his twin sons, now grown to adulthood, and a local Indian community that listened to his stories, cherished his wisdom, and cared for his needs until he passed on in May 2014.

Yet for all his wanderings, Darryl—in his imagination, his writings, his stories, and in the deepest part of his soul—never, even for a day, left Hamma'wi, Pit River Country, the land where he was born. Rich in intimate memories and emotional ties, Hamma'wi was also holy land: it was his Jerusalem, his Bethlehem, his Mecca. *The Morning the Sun Went Down* is thus more than a memoir of an individual life: it's an atlas of a spiritual landscape. Each chapter, whether recounting a personal experience, a historical incident, or a story from Dreamtime, is self-contained and always rooted in a defined and named place: It'Ajuma (Pit River), Bo'ma-Rhee (Fall River Valley), Haya'wa Atwam (Porcupine Valley), Goose Valley, et cetera.

Individuals so dominate our modern sense of being that we often name places after people, and Pit river is no exception. A modern map of the area bears names such as Clayton Canyon, Burney Falls, Pittville, McGee Peak, and a host of others. (I can't help but wonder: did anyone ever ask the peak whether it wanted to be named McGee?) In the world into which Darryl was born, in contrast, place defined and named the person. "My native name, Sul'ma'ejote," Darryl once explained, "is an act of culture, referring to the landscape where I was born, on the north bank of Sul'ma'etoje (Fall River, at Fall River Mills)." In a 2007 interview with *Indian Times,* a publication from UC Riverside, he explained his name and his identity in this manner:

> My connection to my mother and to the earth is in the Fall River Valley, there beside the Fall River. Therefore my native name must show that connection. I am Sul'ma'ejote. There is only one Sul'ma'ejote (the river) recognized by the great universal powers. In the recent past all males were named for the landscape of their birth. In this manner anyone would know you, your birthplace, your genealogy, and your history just by your name. Ramsey Bone Blake, at birth, was named Chuta'pu-ki ahew, jui ajijujui. So, instantly one should know who he is and who his people are, and where that mountain is that has seven springs and one of them called Jui ajijujujui (where the water comes up and the moss and grass are always dancing). In this manner the male person becomes an identifiable part of the landscape. So, like my Aunt Gladys said, sweeping her arm around the mountainous landscape, "Our spirits shall endure long after these mountains turn to dust." That gives us tenure un-limited. She also said, "You must have a 'real' name or the Great Powers won't know who to council."

Just how important place was to Darryl was illustrated dramatically during a trip we took together several years ago. It was after the devastating stroke that left one side of his body nearly paralyzed. Ray March, a newspaper editor who lives in the tiny town of Cedarville, located in the Surprise Valley in Modoc County in the northeast corner of California, had launched a literary conference, and he invited the poet Gary Snyder, the geologist Eldridge Moores, the scholar and cultural activist Jon Christensen, Darryl, and me, along with some local poets and writers, to lecture and teach.

Darryl was living in San Jose at the time, and I offered to drive him to the conference. I hadn't seen him in a while, and when one of his sons, now serving as his attendant, dropped him off at our Berkeley office, I was shocked. My mind retained the image of Darryl as he was when I first met him: handsome, lively, and charming, a man of bullish physical strength tempered with athletic grace. The person I now saw was withered and frail, nearly deaf, scarcely able to walk, his once booming voice now hesitant and slurred. It was a warm day, and he was unable to get his jacket off without assistance, unable to take care of his basic needs.

With help, I got Darryl into my car and set off on what would be a seven-hour journey. The first leg of the trip, north through the Sacramento Valley to Redding, was excruciating. He had trouble hearing me, so I had to shout. His speech was so slurred I couldn't understand most of what he said, and getting him in and out of the car for the frequent rest stops he needed was a feat of engineering. For the first hundred miles or so, I was convinced that I'd made a dreadful mistake by offering to give Darryl a ride. Then, Akoo-Yet (Mount Shasta), the spiritual center of the Pit River world, came into view. Darryl struggled to sit straighter so that he could see it better, and he began to talk about the tiny but powerful spirit, Mis Misa, that lived within the mountain and was charged with balancing the world. As he spoke, he seemed to enter a trancelike state, as if taking dictation from the world beyond, his voice gaining force and clarity. Then, reaching Redding and heading east to Alturas, we entered Pit River Country, Darryl's homeland. With increasing excitement, force, and animation, Darryl began describing the sites we were passing. Up that road is where Craven Gibson lived, who used to tell us stories in the old language. Up that road is where Aunt Gladys and Uncle Rufus lived. That pile of rocks was dislodged by Coyote, who was chasing a woman up that hill. At that corner was a bar that served under-age kids. That waterfall has within it a spirit-being with magical powers. That hillside was where women were collecting *apas* roots when a militia attacked and killed almost everyone; my great-great grandmother was one of the few who escaped. In there is where I went hunting for deer with my father. Mile after mile the stories flowed. While I was exhausted from the seven-hour drive by the time we reached the conference site in Cedarville, Darryl walked out of the car with his body more alive, his voice now strong and clear, his being animated, looking youthful, confident, ready to take on the world.

"We were not created so fragile that our spirits can be broken with bullets," Darryl wrote in the opening paragraph of this book. Although referring broadly to his culture, this could very well be said of his life. As many times as the world dealt him a crushing blow, his spirit, nourished and sustained by the land of his birth, remained unbroken. As people gathered around him that day in Cedarville, Darryl seemed to glow with a power outside himself. I was reminded of the accounts of how the old-time Pit River shamans would summon spirit-helpers, the *dinihowis* and *damaagomes,* to assist them in their cures. Darryl had called upon the powers of Hamma'wi, his homeland, and they responded. Annikadel was by his side, as were Kwaw (Silver Fox), Jamol (Coyote), Wa-low-chah (Cloud Maiden). These and other spirit-beings who worked within "The Great Mystery" to sing and dream the world into existence were there to welcome Darryl home. They came for the same reason we all came, to be in the presence of that rare and beautiful thing, an *It'jati'wa,* a real or genuine person. There are few enough of them in the world, and Darryl was clearly among them.

Malcolm Margolin

April 2016

THE MORNING THE SUN WENT DOWN

HAMMA'WI

1988

At Likely, south of Alturas, in the extreme northeastern corner of California, there was a run-down, worn,
and weary white-man's shack. It was, as were my people at that time, dilapidated. Not so long before, in autumn 1868, the U.S. horse soldiers had assaulted a gathering at *Tuwut-lamit Wusche,* later to be known as the
Infernal Caverns, about eight miles from this place.
Military historians still claim that the soldiers broke the
spirit of my people in that action, a military move that
was nothing more than an assault by men armed with
cannon and rifles upon a native people whose defense
was sticks and stones. That maneuver, however, did not
break the spirit of my people. We were not created so
fragile that our spirits can be broken with bullets.

As I peered into the softly glowing, lamp-lighted
doorway of the two-room house, unseen forces im-
pelled me inside. It was breath-warm within, and thick
shadows moved slowly upon the dingy walls. Mottled
people, as worn as the landscape after an invasion, had

gathered. Ventilation would have been welcome; it seemed that half of my tribe was in there.

Everybody was talking or whispering with everybody else, as if I did not exist. Seemingly my people had no idea I had entered the room. They did not look at me. They did not even acknowledge I was alive, as they continued talking intensely among themselves in a variety of dialects. From the thick hum, I picked out a few "American" words.

What a disaster!

I imagined that I would have a warm welcome, that there would be excitement because I had come home. After all, I had been summoned. I had not asked for them; they had asked for me. But my ancient people continued to talk among themselves, not acknowledging me. They were like deer feeding in the shadows of evening; their conversation focused on each other. I did not know what the whole conversation was, but it was finely focused. Then there was a shuffling among the people, and their "talk" took on a suggestion of something deeper than conversation, deeper even than meaning.

Was I being left out as punishment or a reprimand? I could not quite understand their ignoring me. I was in college at the time, and I thought my Elders had called for me to talk with them about education or politics or law and legal matters. Or perhaps they wanted to ask me about the Americans with whom I had been associating. I could not understand their looking away from me, so deliberately and pointedly ignoring my presence.

In this dream—for it was indeed a dream—my people, like the house and its interior, were very poor, much like they are in reality. Some wore clothing woven from twine and bark, some wore skins of rabbits and coyotes and beaver, and some wore "modern" clothing, dresses made from the empty flour sacks that had "Fall River Mills" stamped on them with a picture of Burney Falls. Others wore black dresses printed with tiny white flowers, a red dot in the center of five petals.

I felt so out of place when my mother's grandmother, "Great Grams," looked up at me, obsidian eyes shining. I froze and everybody stopped talking. There was a silence that was thicker than cold butter. I began to get smaller and smaller.

With a long look, longer than necessary, she said, *"Iss. Ni'lladu'wi e·psyu'yayyow. Inamas'at, Iss?"* (Hamma'wi person, white man thoughts to know you person to say?)

Her question sounded like a demand.

Trembling, I answered. "I think I have figured out the white man enough to say."

There was another silence. Then, with deliberation, Great Grams stated, "Think, no. Knowing, yes. *Iss?*"

In the shadows of that old house many ancient eyes peered at me, dancing with the flickering of the candles that created the light and caused intense, multilayered silhouettes on the walls. Intimidated, I felt that I was on trial.

But I also knew that my ancient Elders coming to me in my dream (which was a fragment of their greater dream) had placed a certain amount of confidence in me. They knew from past contact with white people that they could not trust the white man using the American language. But they somehow could trust me. By their presence, their gaze, their silence, they were endowing me with a special trust. They also had special expectations.

A murmur swelled up among the Elders. There were whispers. Dialects of both *Iss* and *Aw'te* languages buzzed and hummed in the soft shadows. The old house breathed. The council moved in ripples and rustles like leaves in an oak forest touched by the west wind.

One of the oldest of the Elders, a person so old he was unknown to me, with flowing white hair and wrinkles on elbows and knees, who was dressed in skins with a skirt of woven cedar bark, asked my Great Grams if I would speak to them in one of our languages. He asked, *"Iss, tollim, atama Kosalekt'wi?"* (Person, all of us to speak in *Kosalekt'wi?*).

I trembled as my spirit rose up and attempted to shield me from my dreadful ignorance. It was terrible; I could not speak to the Elders in a language they could fully comprehend. My confidence wilted.

Then the same Elder asked my great-grandmother why it was that Great Grams thought I could be trusted, and why more than a white man.

Great Grams did not answer him for a long moment, so I decided that I must defend myself. I said in English that it was the intention of the white people to change me and my generation into English-speaking red-skinned beings in order for us to better serve their wants and their wishes. But if we retained our language and customs, and practiced our traditions and ceremonies, we would not fit into their plans.

Not only was the attempt of the white people to change us harmful but the neglect of our Elders to teach us our traditions was equally damaging. In the final analysis, the omission by our Elders and the intentions of the white people together would lead to our destruction as a spiritual nation of people created for a purpose upon earth by Silver-Gray Fox, *Kwaw*, long ago.

After the translation from English into the *Iss* and *Aw'te* languages, a ripple went through the gathering. Again there was silence, yet the eyes peered at me, some of them wondering, some of them pleading, all of them worried. My spirit did not breathe.

I woke up anxious. To this day I wonder about the meaning of the dream. I have a feeling that the spirits of those people are still in that old house, peering out the stained windows, waiting for the time when I approach their council and can answer that I know the manner in which the white people think, and I also know how to "best them."

And I tremble.

CHAPTER ONE

BO'MA-RHEE

1946

Depression, recession, oppression. Daddy just lost his job. Fear and the brother of fear, anger, ruled our lives. Where was Daddy going to get another job?

An argument between Mom and Dad over money came roaring from the house. I remember what Grams (my mother's mother) said about this white man society: "Money is the master." I was in the field behind the house. Looking toward the mountains, I attempted to block out my mother's anger and my father's yelling. It did not work. Thud! A cup or something hit the wall. My six-year-old spirit moved me deeper into the field. But still I could see Mother's eyes flashing from her slender, light-complected face, long black hair in disarray. Eyes that sparkled so pretty when she smiled, now filmed with anger. And I could see Daddy, short and coffee-colored, round face determined, mouth set straight across, trembling, black eyes staring.

Daddy had been killing animals at the slaughterhouse and delivering meat in a big truck we called "The Gray Ghost." It was not really gray, just dingy. Daddy jobless now, the family was in retreat from the rent-paying American society.

When Dad lost his job, we lived at Glenburn in northeastern California, five miles from the place of my birth at Fall River Mills. My brother, Lester (Buddy), was born in Fall River, too. Buddy is dark like Daddy, one shade deeper than chocolate.

We were a large family: Beverly, Cecelia, Sonny, then me, Madge, Kenny, Lester, Iris (Fefe), and Baby Jerry. I don't remember where they each were born, and it really didn't make any difference. We were all going to live forever, so we could find out birth dates and birth places later on.

Because there was little money and no income, we endured many moods of depression: emptiness, arguments, harsh words, mean flashing eyes, deliberate stares off into time and space. The atmosphere was always brittle in the house when Mom and Dad were arguing over money.

During these times I quietly left the house. Although I could hear my brothers and sisters laughing and playing, and our dogs barking as they ran somewhere, having fun didn't interest me. My belly was green-sick from the arguing, and I thought that there must be a way to fix the arguments—somewhere, somehow.

While my brothers and sisters were playing, I thought that I should be working, should be trying to get a job to help bring money home so we could have happiness. Sometimes I sat in the fork of the big cottonwood tree near the old mill, and worried and slept and dreamed. Mostly I wondered if there ever was going to be a time when there were no arguments. The sky was fat and deep blue, troubled blue.

In the distance in all directions, the heat waves made *Bo'ma-Rhee* (Fall River Valley) shimmer, vibrate, like rippling clean water. In the shade, a thick warm-cool. Any breeze would bring freshness; too long between breezes meant excessive warmth. If I had not been worried, I would have simply flopped asleep, straddling the huge limb of the tree as if I was on the back of Cap or Fox. I wished I had an apple, to smell its perfume and taste its sweet surprise. Every apple tasted different, sweetly different, except for the sour ones.

Through the flat green and silver leaves of the poplar I could see across *Bo'ma-Rhee.* Stories the Elders tell of our history came into shadowy focus. In the 1850s *Bo'ma-Rhee* had few white settlers. However, the immigrants wanted the best land, and the soldiers maintained at Fort Crook complied with their wishes. The demands of the settlers and the often deadly response by the Army left my people without land. Any resistance by my people ushered in more military forces. Soon we were treated as wild animals.

Several miles east of the mill was the site of Fort Crook, named after Lieutenant George Crook, who entered our homeland in 1857 with the cavalry and assisted in establishing the fort with Captain Gardiner and the First Dragoons. While the fort was being constructed, the people say, Lieutenant Crook planted within the soldiers terrible ideas of why and how to chastise our people, especially those identified as "renegades." He cultivated hideous thoughts that he had gathered and polished as he marched from fort to fort, from death camp to death camp.

One year, they say, unrecorded except in the memory of my people, (probably about 1858), just over there at the bend of the Fall River, the white people wanted to get rid of the *Iss/Aw'te.* In those days my people had two winter camps, one on the north end and one on the south end of the valley. To the camp on the north end of the valley the settlers and Army personnel took a wagonload of guns and ammunition—and *whiskey.* The Americans told my people that our camp at the south end of the valley was preparing for war, that the young warriors were going to come and kill them. Worried, the Americans had brought guns so the northern camp could defend itself.

Then the same Americans hurried another wagonload of guns and ammunition—and *whiskey*—to the winter camp on the southern end of *Bo'ma-Rhee*. The Americans said that they were bringing guns so the camp could protect itself because the camp at the north end of the valley was going to wipe them out, and that the northern camp already had guns and ammunition. The survivors—those of my people who wintered in the mountains rather than in the camps—called that conflict "The Great Killing."

Yet today around the campfires in the safety of the pines, our Elders say that the soldiers supplied the guns while the settlers supplied the whiskey. Both parties furnished the rumors, and neither found reason to take any responsibility for the destruction they invented.

The guns, whiskey, rumors, and ammunition, glowing like red coals within each camp, caused flames of fear and hatred to leap into the night. Whiskey, igniting that incendiary element within rumor that allows lies to become facts, caused a growing frenzy and the blurring of reason. With every swallow, the burning drink, whiskey, made people *tila-tosi* (insane). Finally, toward morning, whiskey in collusion with rumor caused the two camps to go out to meet in the open field and annihilate each other.

At dawn, as the booming in the field slowed to a few random shots, then silence, the horse soldiers and the settlers rode out to view their handiwork.

The lessons of our history often end at dawn. The fire smolders, and the people turn and shuffle off in silence to their daily challenges, wondering.

LOOKING ACROSS THE VALLEY, I see the church where I once tasted a variety of homemade pies, some in flavors I had no idea existed. Maybe I can make pies, sell them like the church does—and make money. Beside the little white church, my first school. One day when I was in the first grade, we were playing kickball, and a big kid kicked the ball through the schoolhouse's front window. That explosion still ringing in my ears, I ran all the way past home out into the wheat field and sat behind a big, black corner fencepost.

I knew the sheriff was coming to get us all, and if I had to go to prison, I was not going to surrender on "their" terms. However, hunger and a quickly falling sun made my resistance fade a little. I slowly walked homeward as the sun lingered blood-red upon the mountaintop before falling over the edge of my world. I was thinking all the time that the sheriff's posse was at my home waiting for me in the yard, horses blowing. The posse and the sheriff had shining badges, white-hot pistols, and a rope they intended to hang me with. "Stretch his neck," my uncle would say.

My heart beating fast and my knees trembling, I shuffled home under the cover of approaching darkness. The sheriff was not there. Somehow my life had been spared.

I shifted my gaze. Near "my" cottonwood tree and two hundred yards from our small white house was the huge, gray-brown, abandoned mill. Inside there were massive circular bins that, with much effort, we spun like a circus attraction. Then, tired of spinning, we jumped from one floor to the next, or leaned out the highest window as far as we possibly could. Our mill had several floors. Its rafters fluttered with cooing pigeons and cheeping wrens. Sometimes a robin would land on a window with a dirt-caked worm wiggling in its beak, or a woodpecker would hammer away, digging for insects. Our mill smelled abandoned, but it also smelled like an ancient, dusty playhouse—and it was all ours.

While we played, our band of dogs ran around the old mill chasing ground squirrels. Flashing like earth-colored shadows, the squirrels darted under neglected and weathered lumber or between the cracks of the aging building. When the squirrels vanished, the dogs would abruptly stop chasing and, outsmarted, assume a quizzical look. One old dog had its right ear flopped up and over its head, revealing a pink underside. Another had its lip folded back on a dry tooth. They looked dumb for a moment, forgot about the squirrels, shook their ears, hair, and lips back into position, then went off searching for something else to chase.

When we came down from the upper mill floors, kids and dogs raced amidst clouds of dust in the afternoon sun. Destination not yet established.

Straddling the limb in the cottonwood tree near the old mill, I recalled many stories my people told. One of my favorite storytellers was Uncle Ramsey, who was married to my father's great aunt, Lorena. He said that on the antelope plains before entering Dixie Valley (south of Fall River Valley about twenty miles) there is an oblong and tapered rock formation. There, *Napona'ha* (Cocoon Man, who later turned into the night butterfly and was one of the creators of the universe) killed the king of the *Qwillas*, the alligator dragons, then ordered the rest of the *Qwillas* to the south land forever. That is why there are no dinosaurs or alligators in the land of my people *Iss/Aw'te* (Pit River/Hat Creek-Dixie Valley). As a child I wondered why *Napona'ha* didn't attack Lieutenant Crook and all of the rest of the army at the fort.

Then I remembered the Elders telling that over there, just eight miles past the treetops, a war rampaged long ago, long before time. The Klamaths came down to our country and took from us a Grinding Pestle (representing the labor of the women), a Sky Knife (a long knife made from obsidian and representing warriors and the defense of the people), and a Diamond (representing the wealth of our nation). The Diamond is the luckiest stone in the universe, according to the narratives of my people. "Luck" is something that is very important to our people, a necessary element of life.

Using special powers, *Napona'ha* dreamed that the Pestle, Sky Knife, and Diamond were in the camp of the Klamaths. He went to the mice brothers, twins who are mischievous but able to get out of trouble easily. *Napona'ha* told them to go north to Klamath and retrieve the tribal materials. The twins obeyed *Napona'ha's* instructions, went to Klamath, and returned with the stolen property.

However, the Klamaths sent a warrior who announced to the council gathered at *Napona'ha's* ceremonial house that they wanted to go to war over the Pestle, Sky Knife, and Diamond that the mice brothers "stole" from them. A terrible war raged in the valley while the mice brothers mediated between the warring sides. Finally, *Iss/Aw'te* defeated the Klamaths. The Klamaths returned to their homeland, promising never to enter our homeland again to fight over the Sky Knife, the Pestle, and Diamond. *Napona'ha* and *Iss/Aw'te* constructed piles of rocks both in the timber and in the field to show throughout eternity where this event occurred. They intended for this site to be a lesson in history and for the rock piles to remain as the proof.

Unfortunately, immigrants destroyed the rock piles, cut down the timber, set down posts, and stretched barbed wire fences. After all this, they placed "No Trespassing" signs every quarter mile along the fence. I still wonder how a person who is trespassing upon the land of my people feels when he hammers a "No Trespassing" sign onto a post on *our* land, the origin of *our* existence, *our* Mother Earth, *our* home. My old grandmother on my father's side said sadly, "Some people don't have no shame."

But I should not be thinking and remembering. I should be working. I should have a job.

Listening carefully through the hum of bees and the buzz of little flies and mosquitoes hovering in the shade, I heard the water rushing through the Great Canyon just west of my birthtown, Fall River Mills. Oh! for a clean drink of spring water.

Uncle Ramsey said the Great Canyon was made by a huge fish that got its power from the top of *Ako-Yet* (Mount Shasta).

As I remember, Uncle said that in the beginning, *Kwaw*

(Silver-Gray Fox) forgot to make a place for the powerful *It'Ajuma* (Pit River) to flow. So, *Kwaw* appointed a huge fish to ram the solid rock mountain with its head until there was a canyon for the water to flow to the sea and for the salmon to come to the people during the appointed times, such as when the Old Salmon Singers talked to the waters and sang to the power of the universe. They sang, and salmon came splashing up the mighty river. Uncle wanted to sing the song for us, but he had forgotten it.

In the middle of the Great Canyon is a huge waterfall, *Inalah-Haliva*, meaning "Where the salmon turn back," or "Where they struggle to get up under the water and over the falls, but can't." It was said in the old times that the salmon came here and could go no farther. They spawned and perished, and were used to feed other life forces near the river. The people also gathered the salmon and dried them over a smoking fire for food during the long winter or used the smoked fish as items for trade.

At the western end of the canyon, at the confluence of the Hat Creek and the Pit River, it is said there was much trading. During the salmon runs, the Shoshonis, Paiutes, Klamaths, Wintus, Yanas, Yahis, and many other nations gathered there, at a place called *Ticado Hedache* (The World's Heart). There was singing and dancing, bartering and gift-giving. Medicine exchanged for song and dance. Deer and bison hides for salt. Salt for obsidian. Obsidian for turquoise. Turquoise for beaver and mink pelts. Arrows and bows for beads and silver bells. (Silver bells came from "down below," meaning some place south of our ancestral homeland.) Silver bells for brass. And so it went. The salmon, answering the singers, not only issued a signal to all of the nations to gather and to trade at *Ticado Hedache*, but made the bears return to the rivers, the eagles gather in the nearby forests, and the otter and the mink slip through the shining evening waters seeking fresh salmon or the trout that follow the salmon. The salmon, making the river alive, made the land vibrate with all other forms of life. It was so good.

It was there, too, that Old Coyote taught the people who came to fish how to sing and dance, lightly touching the earth with his toes like summer raindrops. As he sang the magic song and tapped the earth, worms surfaced, and the people gathered them and caught plenty of fat fish. But jealousy over a woman made Old Coyote mad, so he took his song and his dance and left. Now there are no worms, and the people cannot catch many fish.

I watched as our dogs chased a rabbit through a newly harvested field, late-afternoon heat waves causing them all to blur in the distance. The younger dogs yapped on the heels of the rabbit. Rabbit leaped, dove, and disappeared. Reappearing, it made a huge S run across the field. Old Dog followed, going from one tip of the S straight across to the other tip. She caught the exhausted rabbit at the end of the S. Dust, snarling, and confusion exploded. Rabbit was in their blood now.

Just a little later, geese flew across the valley, their forlorn yet beautifully lonesome call amplified in the quiet. Ducks on whirring wings darted through the new evening, heading for the lake to rest upon the safety of the waters, hidden in inaccessible solitude among the tules. They appeared so innocent while in flight, their wings whistling. I wondered why people wanted to kill them. *Chool* (moon), a white shadow, climbed ever so slowly in the silent sky. Maybe *Chool* was worried, too.

It was early summer. The white farmers had already harvested one field of wheat, and soon they would harvest all of them. They looked at us children with ugly eyes. There seemed to be only two times when the white people tolerated my people: when we were in retreat, or when we were dead. I wanted to get away from them.

WHILE WE CHILDREN were in bed, Mom and Dad talked softly. In quieter moments when the argument had faded away, Mom and Dad talked about my favorite topic, our horses, Cap and Fox. Horse-talk was sweet compared to arguments. The excitement in the very suggestion of the names of the huge, powerful workhorses made goose bumps all over me. Somehow the horses always smelled like freedom. Working or running, their muscles and sinews vibrated like bowstrings beneath their sorrel skin. Their black manes shone as they snorted. They were in command of their place. They ate whole apples with one crunch, sweat foamed between their legs, and the perfume of grass was upon their breath. Maybe they could even fix our damaged life, somehow. At my friend Rich's home there was a book on the table with a picture of a flying horse. It was magic. Maybe all horses were magic.

We were in our little rented house in Glenburn, and Mom and Dad were at the kitchen table making plans over coffee. Almost like a whisper I heard "Cayton." Cayton! The Old Home Place. Are we going there? I listened intently. The wind moved softly. My brothers and sisters, all eight of us, jammed under the same quilts, breathed softly. I listened, hoping the changing winds would bring more news about Cayton.

It did not. Six years old and still needing a job, I slept a hard sleep.

CHAPTER TWO

HAYA'WA ATWAM

1946

One Saturday we went to visit some friends over across the Fall River. It was daylight when we crossed the old wooden bridge. Enormous trout darted and flashed below, and sucker fish turned and whipped their bodies to keep pace with the river as they dug the bottom and searched beneath the rocks. A pair of ouzels darted down the river in flight, stopped, vanished beneath the water, magically appeared on a rock across the river, then fluttered back upriver again. The shade of huge trees made it cool near the river. Just upstream the river gushes, freezing cold, from between the lava rocks. Our Wise Ones say it is the place where an underground river emerges, a river that begins inside of *Ako-Yet* many miles to the north.

In a cloud of red dust our old car hammered and bumped along a rough and rocky driveway. Once Dad turned off the engine, the car coughed, and steam hissed and blew more red dust. The earth turned almost black where the boiling water splashed over. Kids spilled out of the old, black automobile, tumbling, excited. We were visiting the Evanses: Stressley and his wife, and all the kids! Dad and Stressley worked on our car while the women went into the house to begin making coffee for the grown-ups and food for the kids.

Although it was exciting being with all the children, I kept wondering how I was going to make some money so there would be fewer arguments around our home. Almost with reluctance, I ran to catch up with the rest of the kids darting over the lava rocks and flashing through the forest in pursuit of a dog or in pursuit of each other. A kingfisher, blue and proud, flashed upstream, spun in midflight, and landed on a limb. It is good luck to see a kingfisher. "I saw him first!" "No, you didn't, I saw him first!" Kingfisher, a blue streak, darted away.

Soon we were all eating. I do not recall whether the children got most of the food or if the dogs did, but we somehow all received enough nourishment to survive. Then, with the sun long down and the candles barely visible in the old windows of the Evans home, it was time for us to move out.

In the powdery darkness of the towering pines and the deep shadows of the black mountains, both families rushed: the Evanses to get their excited children inside the house, and Mom and Dad to get us excited kids inside our car. The usual way of keeping track of us all was for Mom to "count noses." After all of the kids were wrestled into the car, Mom would count the noses of the children to make certain that all of us were accounted for. The number of "noses" now matched to the number of offspring, the door was slammed shut, and the old car slowly turned, like a porcupine, and ambled out of the driveway, headlights flopping, heading for the creaking bridge, the oiled dirt road, and home. The headlights made long orange images and deep black shadows, and *Chool* raced us just on the other side of the trees.

Arriving home, Mom and Dad were surprised to find that one of the Evans girls, Jeanie, was somehow mistaken for one of our "noses" in the count, and one of us must have been asleep or hiding in the car—or something. All accounted for, Jeanie stayed with us that night, and we hurried her home in the morning. The forest around their home beside the Fall River has never heard such laughter. Jeanie home safe, we returned to our place and applied ourselves to the business of survival.

Going to get Daddy's last paycheck, we dropped down from the little hills, crossed the Fall River Bridge, and drove into the town of Fall River Mills. Just across the bridge is the gas station. Hugh Brown, the owner, always gave all of us kids lollipops, whether Daddy bought gas or not. It was automatic: We arrived, Hugh handed us suckers. We liked to go to Hugh's.

Hugh's gas station smelled of oil and old car parts, worn tires and exploded inner tubes. Old men seemed to hang out there all the time, sitting in the office playing a game that required a long board with holes on its surface that they placed wooden matches in. It never interested me. What worried me is that they never seemed to have a job. On the strength of his final paycheck, Daddy charged some gas. I liked to see the gas pumping up into the glass cylinder before it emptied into the gas tank of the car.

Our mouths dripping with sucker juice, we left Hugh's gas station and crossed the Pit River Bridge to the slaughterhouse to get Daddy's last paycheck. Daddy was on good terms with the people he worked for. They smiled when parting, and years later they still seemed to be very good friends. Now Daddy was laid off, and we were almost without a home, yet he smiled and thanked the people who laid him off! I wondered how it was going to be when I was laid off from my first job.

Now Daddy had his last check. He wanted to take a ride up Six-Mile Hill, skirt Hogback Ridge, go to Cassel, then to Highway 299 East, circling the Great Canyon. In that canyon, it is said, Old Coyote heard the song of a beautiful woman long ago. He ran too hard trying to get her to have sex, and he almost fell.

You can see today where Old Coyote "ran outta land" and turned to scramble back up the side of the cliff. There is a place where rocks have been jarred loose.

The plan between Mom and Dad was for Daddy to go to Cayton, the old home of my grandfather Adam Carmony, about seven miles north of Glenburn. There he would turn the soil, revive the old house (May abandoned the house soon after Adam died), and make the barn livable for the horses, Cap and Fox. A blue-white flash, something hurt within my six-year-old being, and I wondered: When was Daddy coming home? What if something happened to him? What if a bear got him? What if he got lost or something?

After I heard the plan, I worried. The other children were asleep under a huge pile of quilts. A piece of old carpet lay crumpled in the corner on the floor. In the darkness, I crawled under it, still wearing my ragged Levi's and my black-and-gold checkered long-sleeve shirt. There, I tried hard to sleep.

For a long time I could see nothing. Then, black shadows turned softer. The deep blue-blacks slowly emerged through the ebony as objects in our home—a doorknob, a chair, the corner of a window took shape. Outside, the dogs were beginning to stir as daylight neared. Another day in my jobless life....

I must have dozed. "Little Herman! Little Herman! Where is my boy Babe? Babe!" Daddy was calling for *me!* And he called me "Little Herman" for the first time, just like other people did. I guess because we looked alike. That's what they said, anyhow.

Coffee was percolating on the old stove in our little house. The aroma was steamy and thick with no beginning or ending. It permeated everywhere. So did the smell of bacon! I threw the old carpet off and ran to Daddy.

"Today, son, we are going to have to assume the responsibility for all of the family." Daddy looked directly at me, deep brown eyes meeting deep brown eyes. I did not understand. "We are going to Cayton this morning, to the Old Home Place," he said. I hesitantly crawled up into my father's lap, not knowing what *responsibility* was or where it was, but assuming command of *responsibility* nevertheless.

Our old automobile was going to stay with Mom and the family. Daddy and I were to ride Cap and Fox over the pass from Fall River Valley to *Haya'wa Atwam* (Porcupine Valley) in Cayton Canyon, to Grams's land. I was so happy.

Soon after breakfast we began saddling the huge horses. The leather smell from the saddles always reminded me of the brand-new cowboy boots in the store in town. These were horses bred to work, big-boned, thick-muscled, wide. They shivered from sheer power. I shivered from sheer excitement.

After throwing me up into the saddle on Cap, the gentler of the two, Dad climbed aboard Fox. The adventure made all of my worries melt. I was taking on responsibility, whatever that was. I don't know if I said good-bye to any of my brothers or sisters, or even to Mom. Daddy, me, and Cap and Fox turned north. It would be a dusty seven-mile ride.

Stretched across the saddle, which was stretched across a very heavy-boned and healthy workhorse, my leg muscles soon began to ache. The rock, plod, bump, rock, plod, bump was almost too much. It didn't take long for some of the excitement to vanish. After an agonizing time, we stopped to pee in the perfumed shade of a ponderosa pine forest. Daddy put me in front of him on Fox, so I was straddling only the saddle horn. It was hard but much more comfortable. I was still in control of Cap: the rope that was his hackamore was now tied around the saddle horn. I felt sort of *responsible*, at least.

We plodded down the red-chalk road, skirted Lake Britton, and, reaching the highway, crossed it with a hurried clop, clop,

clop of the horses' hooves. We turned northeast, staying close to
the railroad tracks, traveling in deep, lush grass. In the clearing
and through the glaring sun, we could see the hill that the old
house rested on, but we could not yet see the roof. In front of us
was the low ground, filled with silt and tules and damp grass. In
the tules, muskrats, frogs, turtles, ducks, and geese gathered. Somehow it just felt comfortable. I was safe. I was responsible and safe
with Daddy, and we were *home*. I was so happy, again and again.

Arriving at the Old Home Place, a quick look around showed
us that the old house required much attention. The roof needed
patching; the front door hung askew with the top hinge pulling
away from its frame; windows were broken. Inside the place was
strewn with old clothes, boxes, and junk. It smelled like very old
newspapers that somebody had peed on. Rats and bats—and
snakes and spiders. Can't sleep in here!

That night Daddy and I sat around a little fire and ate *wa'hach*
(pan-fried bread) brought from our Glenburn home, along with
beans warmed in a tin can and the sweetest apple of my dreams.
That night we slept out on a little hill near the house. Daddy
showed me the North Star, the Big Dipper, the Milky Way. He
talked softly about the universe, about darkness and light, show-
ing me, near the horizon where the sun went down, the evening
stars.

"Come on son, it's time to get up." Daddy already had the fire
going. I jumped up, trying to appear totally prepared to take on
responsibility, wherever it was. My feeling was that it might be
growing pretty nearby, close to a medicine plant.

Daddy threw some more wood on the fire. Then we took the
.22 rifle and went up near the spring. He knew *ha'ya'wa* (porcupines) lived there. There were several in the nearby trees. He fired,
and after a few moments one dropped to earth, thud. He picked
it up by the long claws of its left hand, and we hurried back to the
fire. As I followed, I kept a wary eye on that animal that grew way

over a million needles and could throw them a mile! At least that's what Old Uncle said that he heard, one time up near Alturas.

Being a butcher, Daddy magically sliced the porcupine here, then there, then pulled the entrails out. He chopped some onions, potatoes, and carrots that we had carried over the pass in a paper bag. He threw some salt and pepper inside the cavity of the porcupine, then worked in the whole mixture he had chopped up. Finally, he took a piece of baling wire and sewed the porcupine closed. I watched carefully, but still don't know how he kept from being poked to death by a million porcupine quills.

Next he scooped the coals from the fire pit, put the porcupine in the pit, belly up, laid some dampened oak leaves on the belly where he had sewn the animal together, then covered it lightly with dirt and threw the glowing coals back on top of it all. We then went to the barn, harnessed the horses, and took them, harnesses jingling softly, on the old road down to the field to pull the rusty plow.

The team all hooked up, we began laboring. Daddy made it look easy. Cap and Fox pulled and he aimed the plow, turning the black, mushroom-sweet loam. Meanwhile, I was walking along, picking up worms for fishing, and searching everywhere for responsibility.

For some reason, about noon, I remembered the porcupine and panicked. I thought it must have been all burned up. I threw a clod of dirt in front of Daddy, between him and the horses. He hollered "Whoa," leaning back and pulling on the reins. With a sigh and snorting through their huge lips, the horses stopped.

"Ha'ya'wa! Ha'ya'wa! Daddy! The porkey-pine! The porkey-pine!"

He laughed, unhooked the horses from the plow, tying them to a nearby scrub oak where they could both water and eat. We then hurried up the hill to the fire pit and our porcupine, which

I was certain had burned to an absolute pile of nothingness. We approached the fire. I could see that it was out, not even smoking. Daddy scooped off the dirt and dusted the powder from the expired coals. Where the leaves had been piled on the porcupine's belly, the hair was barely singed. Where the coals had come directly into contact with the quills and the skin, they had crusted like bubbly pork rinds, with the texture of charred leather.

We broke the porcupine open, discarding the plasticlike, burned skin, and began eating the dark, sweetly scorched meat. Lightly salted, it was sooo good! After eating that meal cooked in "the old way," Daddy reburied the porcupine in the pit, then we went back to work with the horses and the plow, turning the earth for a few more hours.

Eventually, I had a can half full of worms for which I felt responsible. Quitting work, we took the horses back to the barn, unharnessed them, led them to the water trough, watched them drink deeply. After retiring them, we went back to the fire where Daddy dug up the porcupine again. It was still hot! Like starved coyotes, we ate again. After dinner I wished for a Baby Ruth, a chocolate candy bar with caramel and nuts. I thought if I wished hard enough, the Baby Ruth would appear just like the apple did. I could eat it while Daddy and I silently fished. The Baby Ruth did not appear. We slept that night on the little hill again. I knew a great deal about stars already, so I slept soundly.

MORNING, EARLY. "We are going hunting or fishing today, son. Gotta give the horses a rest. Just like when our bodies get tired, you can't work 'em too hard next day. Might stop working on us if we get 'em too tired." I bet Cap and Fox liked to hear Dad say that.

So before noon we were sitting comfortably beside the calm waters of one arm of Lake Britton. It was both sunny and shady there, warm and cool. We fished silently for a long time. I was impatient with the results and kept wanting to pull in the line and check the worm. Daddy cautioned me to be quiet. Without even a whisper, a flock of canvasback ducks, their brown-red heads all pointed in the same direction, floated by us, parting the mirror surface of the lake. They slipped around some tules. Their ripples on the lake's surface vanished. I wondered if I had really seen them or if they were part of a dream.

Very slowly, our fishing line moved. Daddy said, "Pull 'er in!" I pulled. There was no give, no fighting. I pulled harder, bending my pole. Whatever it was, it wasn't coming up! I pulled and pulled again and soon tired of the operation. Daddy took the fishing pole, set it aside, and grabbed the line. He pulled long, hard, and slow. Something moved toward us very slowly. "Must be an old limb," Daddy said. Up it came. Slowly, slowly, slowly.... It was close now. Then out of the depths floated a wide and flat, light-brown turtle, the worm still dangling from its hawk-like beak. Its little eyes blinked and its paws clawed awkwardly to get away.

We wrestled the turtle out of the water. "Careful! If he snaps he might cut your finger clear off." I jumped far back, one hand holding the other, thinking that I would rather have all of my fingers for the rest of my life. "Can we eat 'em?" I asked. "Um humm," was the reply. But we didn't. Daddy etched the date on the turtle's shell with his knife, then turned him loose. Then we left for an undisturbed fishing hole around a bend in the lake.

Deer came to drink as we sat quietly nearby. They simply appeared, their huge ears ever alert, tails twitching, the yearlings dancing. Daddy used slight head and eye gestures to point out the variety of life surrounding us. High in the blue, buzzards lazily turned. Above the lake's silver mirror, an osprey swooped down, hit the sleeping surface with a violent splash! He emerged even before the exploded water began arching back to earth. Powerful wings flapping, he moved slowly skyward with a large, desperately flopping silver fish. I watched astounded, awed by almost everything in nature.

It would be more than a week before the rest of the family joined us, so Daddy decided not to kill a deer. We could not eat it all and a lot of it might spoil unless we took the time to cut it in small strips and dry it. However, we didn't have enough time for that process. We "mucked out" the old house, throwing piles of trash out the back door. Daddy hammered boards back into place. We wanted to fix the broken windows, but there was no extra glass within a hundred miles. The door hinges were rusty, and the boards were rotting away. In the barn we managed to find some lumber that had been protected from bad weather. We used it to patch the rotted places. For two days we burned piles of debris. Next, we mucked out the old spring and cleaned the ditch so the water ran from the spring to the house. Soon we had running water, at least to within twenty feet of the front door!

Next we planted potatoes. We cut the potatoes into four or five parts, dropped them along the furrows, then covered them with the dirt turned by Cap and Fox and the now shining plow. All we had to do was wait to eat. The wait would only be until autumn....

Finally, we hammered and banged and sawed away at the old barn, patching it up. I am sure we disturbed the owls, snakes, lizards, and bats, but we had to get the place ready for the livestock and the family.

One day our old car came lurching down the hill. It stopped with a snort like a tired horse. Kids exploded from the doors and windows, curiosity their guide. My brothers and sisters scrambled in every direction. Smiling, Mom ran to Daddy. I know she felt good to be home because a different sweetness wrapped around her.

In the months that followed, we survived because of Daddy's hunting and fishing skills and because he found occasional labor. Two timber fellers came in and cut down all of the big trees on our land. They cut them into logs, and huge trucks took the logs away. The timber fellers were a Chickasaw and a Choctaw. We wondered why they were way out here working when they came from the East, far, far away. What happened to the money for the timber has also been a wonder all these years. Like the trees that became logs, then disappeared, so too did the money.

Summer slowly turned to autumn and an old fear filtered back into my life. I could feel it but I did not know what it was, for sure. Then it came to me. "No! Not school, again!" The thought of being confined in a square room all the rest of my life plagued me.

Our school was at Four Corners, but since there seemed to be only three corners in the little settlement (a place laid out like a Y or a turkey track), we secretly changed its name to "Jack Rabbit Flat," even though there were already a half a dozen other Jack Rabbit Flats in our *Iss/Aw'te* native homeland. One road, Highway 89, went toward Hat Creek and Burney, another road went toward the Pacific Gas and Electric (PG&E) dam at Pit #4 Power House, and the third road went back to Highway 89 toward Burney Falls, Lake Britton, and our home, then on past to Mount Shasta.

It must have been more than a mile and a half from our school to the Lake Britton Bridge, and another mile from the bridge to home. It was probably not more than three miles from home to school the way we went across country. If we followed the main road, looping through the landscape, the journey would be six miles long.

On school mornings, we walked west on the abandoned railroad tracks, and, after crossing Lake Britton Bridge, we climbed the steep chalk bank to the top of the ridge following a well-established deer trail. At the top of the ridge, the land flattened, and we meandered through a beautiful forest until we reached the main road again. The school was straight ahead.

After school, laughter again came from our spirits. We played hide-and-seek in the forest, using fallen logs and caves as our hideouts. We gathered as many of us as we could on a horse's back, and usually got scraped off in a howling pile when the horse darted beneath a low-hanging branch. Family and friends came and visited, bringing more laughter. We played "Stagecoach," with Cap and Fox pulling the wagon, and Sonny, my oldest brother, playing the driver. Some of us played Indians, and our baby sister, Fefe, usually was the "passenger." We raced through the forest in wonder at all of the life.

CHAPTER THREE

DOSE!

1946

Instantaneous hunger gripped the family every day at the same time, sundown. Our hunger was fed by the excitement of living at the Old Home Place, and the thrill of our new freedom. There was no food and it seemed that it was up to Daddy and me to solve that problem, too. Now that the whole family was together again, and there would be no wasting of meat, it was time for Daddy and me to get a deer. Like wolves, we had to eat meat.

Preparing to hunt in the old way, Daddy and I built a small fire down behind the barn that evening. The flames painted Daddy's dark face with deeper shadows, alternating with dancing bright orange. And orange glinted off of his straight black hair.

As a part of our hunting ceremony, we "smoked" ourselves, sparks reaching up into the night when Daddy placed "medicine" in the flames, a mixture of leaves and bark from a variety of trees and shrubs. His brown eyes flashed orange as he looked deep into the fire. Then, after putting the fire out, we went into the barn to sleep under the hay. This was so the *dose* (deer) could not smell the human odor very well. Outside, the black sky was almost white with millions of stars. Inside the barn, sweet dust floated in the old air. *Suk'ahow* (owl) in the rafters returned a call from *suk'ahow* upon the hill.

Now that we were somewhat "cleansed," Daddy said to sleep and to dream about the *dose* we would get tomorrow. "Dream and 'see' them tonight just as they will appear tomorrow. To dream and not see the *dose* is a sign that we should not go hunting. We could go hunting, but we never would come close."

I was almost seven and thought that I was a great warrior. Maybe like Straight Arrow. He taught everybody how to hunt and survive by leaving instructions on a big card in the cereal box. I could read every word, so I learned a lot from Straight Arrow. And I bet I could do everything he said.

But still there were some things that worried me. I knew the contents of the old barn. There were pigeons and hawks, owls and crickets. There were spiders and ants. There were lizards and *how'ta* (rattlesnakes). Some things still frightened me. At those times I was not a warrior after all.

Daddy seemed to go to sleep quickly. Under the hay, I did not rest because I could feel a *how'ta* sliding silently toward me, drawing nearer and nearer. I knew he was there, staring at me. Even though I could not hear or see him, I could "feel" his presence, like a ghost. He was planning to strike me, to poison me to death, then swallow my blood. I was a warrior. I could not wake Daddy talking about a little thing like a *how'ta*, even if it was twenty feet long, and hungry!

I did not sleep for a long time. *Suddenly* dose *appeared, breathing and studying its world with huge eyes that seemed to be made of black glass. It was alert, and puffs of steam came from its nostrils. It was a beautiful doe with huge ears, but it seemed like it did not make any difference if we killed her or not. It was a feathery dream.* Dose *just kept walking away, deeper into the forest and over the hills, then vanished.*

It was still dark when Daddy woke me up. As quietly as we could, we made our way out of the old barn and into the early darkness. At first light we moved toward Lake Britton. Silver shimmered upon the horizon, yet darkness wrapped all around us, thick. We stopped and gathered skunk berries and leaves, rolled them between our hands, crushing the odor out of them, then rubbed the mixture all over our Levi's, hands, shirts, and hair. Daddy always wore Levi's. I did, too. He liked to wear his gray sweatshirt, but I didn't have one, so I wore my long-sleeved, black-checkered shirt with a tear near the pocket.

"Daddy, we smell like *ha'yanna* (skunk)!"

"Shh. In the quiet, everything can hear the human voice."

Obeying the rules of the hunter, silently, without breaking a branch or turning a leaf, we melted into the thick darkness, sneaking west through trees and buck brush. Daddy made no noise. But I often stepped on a dead branch that cracked in the silence of early morning. We stopped, waiting for nature to resume its composure. Then, after tiptoeing for what seemed to be a hundred miles, we heard the wind moving in the forest near Lake Britton. Daddy knew the trail that the deer used as they came early to water from the high country, following the backbone ridge and dropping down the chalk bank. Then the trail skirted the lake.

If I breathed too hard, steam came from my mouth, wisping up into the darkness. Better stop breathing. Creeping now, like two shadows, a big one and a little one, we eased into our position between the sleeping lake and the deer trail. "Get comfortable, son. We may have a long wait."

Silent and motionless, we waited. Long we waited. It seemed like years instead of hours. Still we waited. I was uncomfortable and wanted to change position just a little, but was afraid I would make a noise and everything would hear me, and the deer would run away.

Then! Daddy tensed slightly. "*Dose,*" he whispered softly. The urgency in Daddy's voice was a command, signifying several very important things. It meant for me to be quiet, like stone. It meant that the *dose* we dreamed of and were waiting for had arrived. It meant that I must use all of my hunting and warrior power to remain silent, now that we were within reach of our game. It meant that now the family would eat, and if I made a noise, if I breathed, if I in any manner spooked the *dose* and they took flight, I would be responsible for our family having no food.

His rifle was aimed at the target. Daddy was set.

In the dim light I stared hard, eyes riveted on the place where Daddy's rifle was aimed. Then my heart leaped! I went dizzy and thought I was going to faint. There, magically, almost at the end of Daddy's gun, appeared the *dose* that I had dreamed about last night! It stood motionless, its ears alert. Its eyes peered into tomorrow. Two small mists wisped from its shiny, black nose. It remained frozen as if a statue, its alert, shiny black eyes reflecting the whole morning world.

My spirit screamed, "Shoot! Daddy, Shoot!"

Then, as magically as it appeared, *dose* disappeared. It simply vanished, like the mist from its nostrils, like the *dose* in my dream.

I was confused. We came here to kill a *dose*, and Daddy let it get away without a single shot! I wanted to scream, but remained mute and motionless. I had to. That is the way of the hunter, they always said. Daddy's rifle was still aimed at the target.

Then! The *dose* appeared again! No, this was another one. I thought I had blinked, and the first deer was still standing there. But this one held its head differently. "Shoot! Shoot!" cried my tormented spirit, again and again. In this manner many *dose* passed through the target, none breaking a branch.

Finally, for two reasons, I gave up on Daddy ever shooting. First, I had cramps everywhere. Second, I knew the *dose* would all pass by, and Daddy would not shoot. All the deer would be gone before he decided to kill one. My worried spirit and my aching body both decided that I should adjust my position, just a little. However, my will and the laws of hunting would not allow the slightest movement.

BOOM!

A thundering explosion shattered the quiet of morning. A red splotch came out of my consciousness and turned black, trimmed with silver. Faintly, I heard the rifle report echoing across the lake. The sweet, fresh air was filled with the pungent odor of smoke from the burnt gunpowder.

That BOOM! knocked me back into the thick brush, almost unconscious. I had been numb from waiting, numb from seeing the *dose* of my dreams; now I was numb from the report of the rifle. In the darkness of the brush, I lay there as if I were the one shot and not the *dose*. I tried to move my finger. It worked! Then my arm. Then my legs. Slowly I gathered myself together, and with a loud ringing in my ears, got up and looked around in the early light.

By the time I had recovered my senses and my balance and found Daddy and the *dose*, he already had the animal's stomach open with the hunting knife. Like skinny, dancing ghosts, steam wisped up into the early chill. A salty smell permeated the air. Daddy had blood on his hands, and dark blood clots lumped nearby. And pink blood foamed from its lungs.

Shivering from fright and excitement, and from sitting in one position *forever,* I stumbled around to the *dose's* head. I saw the painful blue-silver glitter of death in its eyes. I felt very sorry for the *dose*. Only a few moments ago it was alive and traveling with its family. Now it was food for our family and for the earth. To kill seemed like committing a crime, a bad one. Especially killing something so pretty. My stomach shook silently. I knew Straight Arrow would not cry, so I didn't either. But I wanted to. Still, again.

I thought about the deer's spirit. Eyes that only a few moments ago had seen the whole world shining now—maybe—saw shadows of memories. Upriver, *ma'ka'ta* (coyote) forlornly yapped to a departing night.

As is the custom of our mountain people, Daddy took out the purple liver from among the mounds of entrails and cut off a small piece for me and one for himself. He called upon *Kwaw* (the Wonder Power that created the universe) to forgive the injury to the family of the deer, and the injury to the silence of morning. Daddy licked the blood from the liver, then, in ceremony, ate it, for now his family could eat.

I looked at my piece of liver. It seemed to be looking back at me. With some hesitation I tasted the blood. I questioned my warrior-spirit, and wondered how Straight Arrow would react. Then I remembered that my grandfather might be nearby, studying me as I grew a little more this morning. Yes, Grandfather was watching me from somewhere secret in the shadows. I could feel his presence. So, in the manner of my people, I put the squishy piece of blood-warm liver in my mouth. A sharp taste (which I have always remembered) attacked my tongue with a vengeance. Saliva flooded my mouth as if I had just bitten a hundred lemons. The soft flesh slipped and slid and did not want to go down my throat. I wrestled with it, and my spirit wrestled with it. Then, finally, it squiggled down. It almost got stuck, then kind of swam toward my stomach. I needed water, quick!

I ran to the lake, flopped down on my belly, and took a big swallow. Then, after waiting a few minutes to make sure the liver stayed down, I returned to Daddy and the *dose*. He had picked the carcass up and wrapped it around his neck so he could hold both front feet in his right hand and both back feet in his left. The head flopped down and the dry tongue hung out.

On the way home we stopped to rest, Daddy leaning against the fork of a tree to support the weight of the deer. He saw my tears.

"Son?"

"'Cause of ... *dose* ...."

Daddy gave me a pat on the head.

"There are many things you must learn. As hunters, we must kill so our family will live. All of nature knows this, and the hunter must obey all the laws of nature. One of those laws, the most important, is to talk with *Kwaw* and set things straight with the Great Powers of the world.

"In a herd that is in a following pattern, one after the other, the first *dose* is always the leader, strong, young. Do not kill this one. It is in nature that the old ones follow last. This is because the last one is the one ready to be taken; its life has been lived.

"Maya'ki, piriki, wer'ak'mita (Wolf, Grizzly Bear, Panther) know of this law, and they obey it. They wait beside the trail just as we did this morning. When the last *dose* passes, they spring to kill, just as we did.

"Don't worry, son. It is a great law that you have obeyed. *L'hepta* (let's go), the family is waiting."

Daddy rocked the deer back to the balance of his body and turned toward home. I was one step behind him, carrying the rifle and the knife that still had blood on it. I felt very important. After all, I had just obeyed a great law, although I didn't quite know which one. Yet something about the *dose* was not settled in my heart. Maybe it was supposed to have another baby? I could not tell.

After walking for a while, Daddy had to rest again. He saw in my eyes the emotions that had broken through to the surface of my being.

"Remember, it is because of nature that the barren doe, the one that can no longer have babies, follows behind the herd. She is a decoy. When we, or the mountain lion, take the last *dose* that moves along the trail, we are taking only one from the world. If we take the first ones, the ones that are still having babies, we do not know how many *dose* we have killed, and we upset the way of life all around us."

"... But, Daddy, *jamat* (a fawn)."

"No, Son, no more fawns. Because this deer is old and it was last. It was not as frisky as a younger doe and its neck is longer. The ears were not as alert and are large and floppy. And since *dose* moved slowly, I knew it was barren. It could not have babies."

Daddy could see all of that in the almost dark? Somehow I understood. And somehow I knew that I had just taken a big step toward becoming *It'jati'wa* (a genuine man). *It'jati'wa* with a great, new, strutting pride.

Arriving home, we created some excitement. Mom and all the kids ran out to see. Even the dogs jumped up and down. They were dreaming about bones, I bet. And I think *ha'yanna* (skunk) and *ma'ka'ta* (coyote) got the guts down near Lake Britton—and the ants got some, too.

CHAPTER FOUR

ELAM'JI

1947

Our old barn this evening somehow took on a mean, confused look. Maybe it was the position of the moon, or the stringy clouds over the mountains, or the owl hooting from the oak forest nearby. We wondered. A strange, heavy thickness permeated the evening as darkness wrapped all around us. It seemed hard to breathe.

Three grown-ups, old friends of the family, were visiting overnight. The adults would go deer hunting before dawn. The adults were smoking and talking, making small plans for the morning. My brothers and sisters and the dogs milled around, and I listened to the adult conversation, thinking that maybe I would be invited to go hunting, too.

We were all outside in the heavy evening, cloaked in hesitation or expectation. The velvet shadows of the trees made me feel like a powder-shadow. I could see my hand move in the darkness, but I could not tell for sure whose hand it was. If I blinked hard, I couldn't see anything for a few seconds after I opened my eyes, except a rainbow pattern that changed and moved, then vanished.

There was a hush. The adults stopped smoking. I could feel all of the eyes studying the darkness.

Then from the old barn, about fifty yards from where we were all standing, a thicker, darker shadow ran down the old barn road that curved below the house and forked out into the meadow beyond. Cold fear streaked up and down my spine, tingling.

The running shadow made no noise. We could barely see its form, and the broken shadows of the oak forest kept blurring it out of existence. Sometimes it disappeared among the darkest shadows. Then the shadow somehow reappeared again, running heavily toward the meadow.

My eyes have always tricked me in the dark. If I looked behind or in front of the fleeing form, I could see it. But if I looked directly at it, I could not. I heard a limb break, but everyone else said they only heard silence. Must have been my imagination.

I could "feel" that spirit as it ran. Why was the spirit running where we could see it? Perhaps it wanted to be seen, to deliver a message. My mother's mom always talked about the mysterious presence of the *Elam'ji*—"the unknowable," "spirit." She was always seeing *Elam'ji* in the blackest part of night. She talked to these spirits in the old language. It seemed that they were present only when she was around. But she was far, far away tonight, clear in Alturas.

An intense chill flashed through me, and I instantly got ghost goosebumps. The hair all over my body stood erect. My knees seemed to lock together. If that spirit ran toward me, I would not be able to move. Maybe I could jump like a kangaroo rat. My body seemed very light. When I tried to move, nothing worked! I was holding my breath and could not breathe. I peered into the darkness, but could see nothing but thick blobs of shadows. Everyone was silent. Listening. Staring.

Finally somebody moved. The grass rustled. A dry oak limb snapped underfoot. There was life! I began breathing again, but it was hard labor, like somebody had tied a rope tightly around my chest.

We were all merely enjoying the summer evening—or were we? Maybe we were secretly commanded by this spirit to be outside so it could let us know that it was alive. Maybe there would be an invasion of these shadowy spirits. My child's imagination raced in so many directions. What if more shadows came? What if they took over? What if they began a war? What if they took us away in the dark?

The old ones say there is a Rock Man roving the land at night. He listens for crying children. He can tell when a child is crying because it is hungry, or because it is wet and needs attention, or because it is brokenhearted or lonely and neglected. It is the brokenhearted and neglected that he takes in the night. In the morning the baby is not there with its mother and father. It is far away.

They say there is another tribe that has "gone on ahead." They are around us all of the time, but we can't see them because they are in another world, the world of Rock Man and other spirits. We can look right through them, we can even run right through them, but we don't know they are there. The spirit-tribe does not allow other people into their world. They speak our language and not foreign languages. They are very smart, that spirit-tribe.

This *Elam'ji* seemed to be heavy, ambling like a massive man, but not making any sound. In my imagination I could see his eyes, blue with moving clouds, like the sky. They must be able to see both in the night and in the light because they *looked*. I had felt that "look" in the forest—that Rock Man look, that spirit-tribe look. It is true, what the old ones say—we are never alone.

Our friends said they too felt something or saw a spirit running down the road below the house. They held their breath, convinced there was "something." We knew we were not imagining this whole episode. In the darkness we stumbled down to the old barn road. I did not want to go along, but I was sure not going to be left alone in the suffocating black silence with an invisible spirit. It was terribly quiet. Only our breathing and our confused visions scraped the darkness.

Somebody lit a match. Flickering orange light. We studied the ground, straining to find a broken limb or bent grass. Maybe freshly turned leaves. Nothing. Another match. Soon there were several matches going. Nothing. All of our senses alert, we listened to the darkness all around us.

We breathed deeply. I wanted to go home and crawl under the bed. That was the safest place in the world, especially if you had a puppy with you. Mine was soft and warm. He liked me. I called him "Boy."

The spirit-thing was gone. Sometimes Grams went out at night and whispered in the old language. She spoke softly, and we could not hear. She did not want us to hear. I believe she was speaking with the spirit-beings.

Somehow I began breathing normally again. Yet every sound in the darkness startled me: a rustling leaf, a breaking twig, the call of the owls. When a breeze moved the oak forest, a shiver ran through my body. I leaned on Mom and stayed close to Dad, trembling. Like a herd of blind deer in the darkness we moved toward the house. I fell over tree limbs and each time I was sure the others would leave me there in the dark, and something would get me.

We stopped. We tensed.

In the blackness above the forest there came a threatening, whooshing sound. It moved slowly across the sky. I knew it was a war battalion of spirits flying in to get us all. I froze. We all did.

My knees were locked together. Neither could I blink. My feet seemed to be nailed to the ground.

The whooshing was overhead now, coming from the east. The east, where many bad spirits originate. The east, beyond the salt waters where the legends say bad spirits dwell.

Then we heard the unmistakable bugle call of the Canadian goose. "Honkers" we called them. Dad's great-aunt Effie called them *hongas*. A tribe of geese was feathering down to land on Lake Britton in the dark. They made a wide pattern like an airplane circling before coming in for a landing. In my mind's eye I could see them. A huge V formation, floating softly down, circling, their black necks and heads slowly moving from side to side as their soft brown eyes studied the waters, the forest, the landscape through the darkness. Their immense wings out and curved, their black feet trailing behind. The wind whooshing their huge bodies forward. So beautiful. Not like the spirit that scared us all—at least, me.

When we arrived at our very dark house, two adults went inside first. I squeezed somewhere in the middle of the frightened tribe. I could feel the darkness in the house with my fingers, like soot. After striking a match, Daddy located a kerosene lamp and lit it. That was better. Light. Warmth. Hope. Maybe the Rock Man spirit-people did not like lamplight. Maybe now they would stay away.

Orange-black shadows danced around the room as the flame from the lamp moved with our every breath. Shadows crept across the windows. In the deep corners, enough dark defied the flickering light to hide a spirit! I did not look into the corners or under the table. I moved closer to Mom and Dad. It was somehow safer next to Daddy. That spirit-being might get me, but Daddy would get the spirit back.

I did not close my eyes all that night. Just stared. Shadows formulated in the total darkness of our bedroom. They oozed across the ceiling like smoke-snakes; they floated and swam around, changing shapes and sizes. And they all "looked" right at me.

"LOQME," OLD UNCLE WOULD SAY, meaning how beautiful the approaching day promised to be. The silver of first light danced off the forest upon the mountains to the east, a sterling silver, a shiny promise. I made it through the night without a spirit getting me. Boy, *loqme*, for sure!

The thick black of our bedroom slowly changed to dark gray, then heavy shadows took form. The ceiling, the door, the chair began to take shape. Soon lots of light poured in. I knew in the light the spirits could not steal me without somebody seeing them, and the spirits knew it.

Slowly, like a just-waking porcupine, I got out of bed, my head heavy without rest. My eyes, open all night, burned dry. My arms and legs ached, since I had been tense and twisted, waiting for a spirit to grab me. My stomach was like a knot in a rope that the horses used to pull a plow. My teeth ached, I had clenched them so hard. I could have bitten a ten-penny nail in half.

The other kids were sleeping, as were the puppies. I shuffled outside to look at the silver sun streaming through the forest. I saw that Mom and Dad and the others had already gone hunting; the hunting knife with the leather handle was gone from its place just beside the door.

I slowly, deliberately worked my way around the house to look down the hill toward the place where the spirit ran the night before. I peeked around the corner, knowing the spirit could not tell if I was there because I was so quiet and small.

As my right eye searched the oak-forest shade more carefully than a whisper, my heart stopped. The ghost goosebumps—ready all the time—jumped up.

There, leaning against an oak tree, "looking" at me, was a soft, silvery, shadowy outline. *Elam'ji!*

I tried to die in order to keep the spirit from getting me. My skin nearly crawled off my body like the snake's does. I was fear-frozen in a staring match with the spirit. He kept looking at me. I was shaking and my knees were locked together again. I could not run.

Then the spirit vanished into the oak tree, like magic. It did not come out the other side. That amazed me as much as it frightened me. Yet my body shivered. My spirit trembled.

Then a calm moved across my world. Like the Elders say, that made me imagine: blue sky was in his eyes and summer clouds there too, clear past the mountains. It was like looking into to-morrow and into the next day.

Why was I trembling? The spirit-beings would not get me. I was not neglected. Mom and Dad loved me. A sweetness moved in and softened the look from the spirit-being.

Maybe it was Great-Grandpa, whom I had never met. He never met me either. Perhaps this spirit was a messenger. The old ones always said the spirits bring messages, if you can understand them. This must be a good spirit.

I soon realized that the spirit was friendly. For some reason I trusted it just a little. I grew. And grew bolder.

LATER THAT MORNING the adults came from the direction of Lake Britton. The men had taken turns carrying the deer. Mom and Reitha were trailing behind, carrying the rifles and talking and laughing softly. Soon we would eat *wa'hach* (bread slowly cooked on a griddle without grease) strong enough to wrap around chunks of *dose me'suts* (venison), along with potatoes fried in bacon grease, eggs over easy, and fresh, cool water.

Hunger made me forget about the spirit. Then I remembered

him again. I wondered why I simply could not forget. Laughter occasionally erupted as the men cut the meat, the women peeled potatoes, and the kids got wood for the fire. Even the dogs were happy. Let the owls hoot in the daytime. We were going to live!

See, I knew the spirit was bringing good luck and not bringing bad warnings. I was confident about life again. But still I wondered why the hair on my neck kept crawling like a lazy caterpillar.

CHAPTER FIVE

NO STAGECOACH!

1946

They were coming too fast!

We (my brothers Kenny and Buddy and I) were the "Indians." Sonny, the oldest of my brothers, was the stagecoach driver. Fefe, the baby girl of the family, was the passenger. The Indians hid along the road that meandered past the barn through the oaks and pines and out across an open hilly place, east from home. We planned an ambush from three strategic points. Out in the flat behind the hills, we lurked.

A fierce thundering approached. Hooves gnawing at the ground, the two huge workhorses, Cap and Fox, were running scared. Although we were supposed to stay hidden and "attack" the wagon train—our family's buckboard—at just the right moment (even though it always got away), we jumped up from our hiding places to see what was happening.

Cap and Fox were running low to the ground, their harnesses flailing the air, tingling, jingling, flapping. They were dragging the tongue of the wagon! Flopping behind them, the tongue frightened them even more. The tongue is supposed to be bolted directly onto the frame of the buckboard. But there was no driver and no buckboard, only a trail of dust. It was like seeing only a part of a car go by.

We always helped harness Cap and Fox, so we knew where all the connections were, how to weave the reins through the proper rings, and how to unite the team with the single tree attached to the tongue of the buckboard. We knew the parts of the buckboard that were removable, and we knew the parts that were designed to stay together. Seeing the tongue of the buckboard dragging behind the horses told us that we would find disaster wherever the rest of the buckboard had crashed.

Cap and Fox vanished east at a dead run. We ran west, homeward, dropping our oak bows and our arrows. We knew the buckboard had to be broken, and we panicked thinking that something terrible had happened. Something really, really bad. Something that cannot be described, but was wrapped in a white, shimmering fear, grabbed and clawed at the pit of my stomach. We seemed to run in slow motion. We did not know what we would find, but surely it must be terrible.

We ran for a quarter of a mile homeward, into the unknown. Not racing each other, but our terrified imaginations. The worst would be somebody dead, blood splattered all over the ground.

From the plains where we had been, the road dipped, then curved up the hill, and finally straightened. The old barn was nestled there in the trees. We always pretended that the barn was the blacksmith shop where the horses got new shoes, were fed, watered, and rested, and the stagecoach was prepared for the next hundred-mile journey into Indian Territory. We imagined, too, that Gabby Hayes was riding shotgun, just like in the movies.

We were getting closer and could see the barn about fifty yards away. No stagecoach! We ran faster!

At the corner of the barn was a huge oak tree. One of the roots grew above ground. Passing the barn, outgoing traffic would pass the oak, swing around it to the left, and follow the road down the curve out onto the plain.

This time, Sonny had wanted to prevent the Indians from taking advantage of a slowly moving stagecoach. He had decided to take the wagon and team up near the house, thereby getting a fifty-yard jump that would send them speeding past the barn, around the oak, down the hill and onto the plain. When the stagecoach hit the plain, it would be going so fast it would fly past the Indians. Gabby Hayes wouldn't even have to use his shotgun. That was Sonny's plan.

Since the old buckboard didn't have a bench, Sonny had to drive sitting next to the passenger on the wide-open flatbed rimmed with twelve-inch oak two-bys. Apparently, as the wagon and team had approached the huge oak near the barn, the front left wheel rolled up the thick root, right up the tree, and flipped the buckboard over flat on its back, breaking the tongue, freeing Cap and Fox from the frame, and landing with its wheels up and spinning like a huge dying insect.

The horses panicked, running faster and faster, until they became frightened shadows darting across the landscape.

Agile, Sonny jumped free of the tumbling wagon and landed safely on the leaves. Unfortunately, the "passenger" flipped over with the buckboard and, being only a toddler, did not know what was happening anyhow. When the upside-down wagon stopped sliding, she screamed.

When we Indians arrived, we heard a muffled squeak beneath the overturned wagon. Sonny broke a dry oak limb off a tree. He placed a rock for a fulcrum and tried to pry the wagon up. It was futile. We were exhausted from our run to the scene of the accident, and the buckboard was too heavy to lift, even for all of us together.

While we labored over the broken, upside-down buckboard in an effort to free our baby sister, we heard a dreadful noise.

It was the old car coming down the road. We all grabbed the

wagon and tried to lift it, but it would not budge. The car approached. Mom and Dad were in the car, and we were in trouble: the baby of the family was trapped under the wagon, and by now she was screaming. We could not know if she was hurt. We knew she was alive, but—

The old car came to a sliding halt in a cloud of dust. Mom and Dad immediately saw the accident. As they jumped out, they slammed the doors of the car, a deadly slam.

We fled. I wanted to go clear across the ocean.

I looked back through the oak forest as Mom and Dad approached the wagon. They thought it was only turned over, until they heard Fefe screaming. Then they were scared, too. Daddy grabbed one wheel of the old buckboard and rocked one side of the wagon off the ground. Mom reached under and got the baby. They were confused and frightened. But then they got angry. Daddy looked around, peering into the forest. We continued our flight to the farthest place in the world that we could find.

From the last time we'd gotten a spanking, we knew that we should all flee in a different direction. Mom and Dad could catch only two of us, so somebody might get away, maybe long enough for them to forget. Buddy, the youngest boy, and one of the Indians, would not get spanked. He was too young. But the other three boys would.

I got away. Sonny and Kenny were caught. I heard them screaming through the oak and pine trees.

It was long past dark when I sneaked back. I crawled under the house and slept with the dogs. In the morning I wanted to come out but could not, even though my hunger demanded that it be fed. I had already been away from the family for so long it seemed that to return now would be like walking into a strange camp where I would be attacked.

The memory of that last time we were spanked was still vivid in my mind. Mom and Dad were gone, and the whole family was playing hide-and-go-seek. We played in a very rough part of the valley, lava flows, deep forests, a cave. It was a wild land where it was easy to find a good hiding place, but many animals liked to hide there, too.

We always imagined that bears or owls lived in the cave, along with bats. Maybe somebody had died in there. We would hide in the dark, and when our eyes could see, we would be next to a skeleton! We knew for sure bats liked skeletons.

Our oldest sister found a perfect hiding place far back in a huge hollow log near the cave. She inched back as far as she could, then touched something soft. It was silky warm. She knew from touching the skins of many animals that it was not a dog or a bear. It was *wer'ak'meta* (panther)!

We do not know how she got out of the log, but there was a high-pitched scream—"L I O N !"—as she fled homeward. All of the "hiders" screamed, as if screaming would somehow keep the lion away from us, and we dashed homeward in a blind panic. Mom and Dad were there. We thundered and screamed toward them. In a panic we told our story, everybody talking at once. Finally, Mom and Dad realized there was a mountain lion out there, and that Fefe, who was "it," was out there still counting at home base.

We all ran toward where she might be. As we ran, I could see images of the mountain lion chewing the very last bite of her. Then the lion would leisurely lick the blood off its hands and its coat. Full, it would be lying on its side in the warm sunlight when we arrived. I thought I would never see Fefe again. I stumbled on as if running in deep cotton.

When we arrived, Fefe was still counting. She was standing alone beside the tree that was "home" in the full sunlight, mumbling numbers as best she could. Mom and Dad cried because she was safe. Then Dad turned around like a grizzly bear poked by a hot iron. We knew we had to flee for our lives again. We scattered like a covey of frightened quail.

He got us all eventually and delivered very good spankings. We understood why: because we left our baby sister out there in the wild with a mountain lion while we had all run home. We did not think about her safety. We thought only about our own. From that time on, I stayed very far away from mountain lions when I was playing.

Now another disaster. Hunger finally drove me to crawl out from under the house. I was going to get a spanking anyhow. But maybe afterward Mom would give me something to eat, or I could knock a piece of jerky off the wire that stretched across the kitchen just to knock the edge off of my hunger. It sure would be good.

As I sneaked into the house prepared to receive the judgment, strong hands gripped me. Daddy! I began to yell and scream, struggling for freedom at the first touch, thinking that somehow if I were pretending pain, the punishment would be less harsh. It was not. I learned that not being responsible can hurt pretty bad and for a long time. However, this time I could not see why. It was Sonny who had been driving the buckboard. So why should I get a spanking? I think it only could have been because I thought only about my own safety.

After the hurt went away, I began to think about food again. Mom and the girls were peeling potatoes. It would be a long time before I had anything to eat. I took the handle of the broom and knocked a piece of dried meat off the wire. The jerky was hard, like chewing old, dry boots, but it was good. I waited for the potatoes, chewing hard.

CHAPTER SIX

HOW'TA DOCTORS OF CAYTON CANYON

⩩

1946

My brothers and I had just heard Uncle tell a story about our grandfather, Adam Carmony, and how he "tamed" rattlesnakes. "Just 'fer fun. Like a mustang, you gotta show 'im who's boss."

Me and my brothers decided to tame a rattlesnake. Inspired to emulate our grandfather, we needed a rattler, badly. In the shade, the four of us waited, frozen into the afternoon landscape. No talking. No moving. No breathing. Sonny was ten, I was seven, Kenny was five, and Buddy was little more than a toddler.

How'ta slid out of the lava rocks and across the dry leaves. He slipped without a whisper into the open. Finally, our chance!

We were rattler-armed. Sonny had a forked "snake stick." Buddy and I were bare-handed. Kenny had socks wrapped around his hands to slow down the strike of the rattler. Sonny's job was to hold *how'ta* by the neck with the forked stick, and we were to grab it with our hands and wrestle it into a gunnysack. "Betcha Grandpa wouldn't use a stick," I thought. Maybe we all thought that. The story Old Uncle had told us about our grandpa Adam and the "taming" of rattlesnakes was so real that it lingered in our thinking, stuck there like a wood tick in the dog's hair.

Only yesterday Uncle was visiting. He had his usual bottle of red wine, and he was, as usual, jolly. The wine made him talk. He always called someone younger than himself "Son." And almost everybody called him "Uncle."

After rolling the bottle up and down his leg, and after a couple of long pulls from his shiny "friend" (accompanied by a hard, sour look), he settled his dark, squat body back into the early afternoon leaves. With his bottle spout he shoved his worn and dirty black hat to the back of his head and began:

"Saw 'im tame a rattler onc't. We brought it in a gunnysack from Six-Mile Hill and dumped it on the ground right about there." He indicated "there" with his bottle, too. "He filled the hundred-pound gunnysack plumb up, maybe more'n six feet long. Its body thick as my thigh. Where his head connected, well, it was bigger'n my wrist. And the head! Son, it was as big as a prizefighter's fist!" He doubled his fist and held it at arm's length.

"The old man looked at *how'ta* a little while, talked to 'im, then gets back, far back a ways, and takes his shoes off.

"'Get 'im mad with a stick,' he says. We do. We gets a long stick and jabs 'im. By now, *how'ta* is one mad José. He's far from home and poked with a sharp stick. He stares at us strangers surroundin' him, coils up, makin' a mound about three feet tall, raises his head, flicks his forked tongue out about a foot, bobs a little, freezes, and stares hard some more, straight at us. He shakes a rattle that is about as long as a tine on a big forked-horn buck.

"We look into his eyes and see a thousand pieces of gold and black, like broken glass. There is no center, just glass that floats and changes places, deep one time, on the surface the next. Then anger. When we feels like we are goin' into them eyes, we draws back, way back!

"The old man's ready. Barefoot, he runs straight for *how'ta*, then jumps clean over him. *How'ta* does not move, maybe a little, but his tail vibrates, and the rattle is a deadly warning, sounded like it came from every direction. Scared me thirty feet away, and I still hold my stick.

"Old Man gets ready again, runs straight for *how'ta,* jumps clean over him again. This time, drags his foot so it hits Mister Rattler in the face, not hard. *How'ta* ducks and dodges and shakes his rattle as hard as he can. They could hear it rattle clean over to Burney. He is madder than ever. His tongue keeps darting out, forked and blacker'n the Ace of Spades at midnight.

"The eyes never blink, staring. The fat head moves slightly from side to side. His coil moves to make sure there ain't no more surprises. *How'ta* bobs 'n weaves his head like a prizefighter." Uncle pretends to ward off blows from the World Champion. "We keep our breath, watchin'. That rattler is cocked deadlier'n a double-barreled shotgun filled with number ten shot.

"The old man gets back and runs again, straight for *how'ta.* This time he kicks *how'ta* smack in the face, hard. Mister Rattler rolls over, flopping. He has had enough and makes a run for it. He stretches across the grass, headed for the hills, but before he can get far, old Adam reaches down and picks him up just behind the head. The long and thick body writhes, rattles vibrate in the leaves and grass. That was a big rattler. Biggest I ever seen.

"Old Man talks to *how'ta* again. He puts *how'ta* on the ground. Rattler moves away. We breathe. Don't know just how long I held that breath." Thirsty from the excitement of the story, Uncle takes another "pull" from his "friend," makes the sour expression, and surveys the area. Maybe he expected to see a rattler.

"Uncle!" Sonny, excited, asked, "Was our grandfather Adam a rattlesnake medicine man? A *how'ta* Doctor?"

"Yes, sir, I'm a-tellin' ya', he was. I seen it. I was there."

MY BROTHERS AND I were stationed in a little forest about two hundred yards above the house where the lava and the trees meet,

when a rattler slid into the clearing, not knowing that it was surrounded by half a tribe that fully intended to "tame" it and become *how'ta* Doctors, "just like Grandpa."

We rushed Rattler from all sides. It writhed and ducked and
made a run for it—just like in Uncle's story. Sonny tried to get
the fork of the stick just behind its head, but it was too quick.
Rattler slithered toward the lava rocks, black diamonds on its
dark back making a dizzy pattern. Its head darted into a large
crack in the rocks, and it was sliding quickly to safety. It could not
turn to strike us because of the narrow area between the rocks.
Sonny threw away his forked stick, then we all grabbed its mus-
cular, desperately writhing body, just like Grandpa probably
would have and pulled it back out of the lava rocks, slowly. Sonny
reached down with his hands and let the rattler slide through as
we pulled, like tugging a big-muscled worm out of the earth, until
the head was just about free. Then he squeezed it a little harder.
Got him! Snake writhed around struggling to get free. It twisted
and slid. Six hands held the snake firm. After a few moments it
ceased to struggle and lay there, subdued.

Our first rattler to be tamed Grandpa-style. Grandpa would
be proud. We didn't need a rattler stick either. Besides, using a
rattler stick to catch a snake was *chicken*.

Resting there in the shade, our hearts finally stopped pound-
ing so hard. Catching *how'ta* was like running a ten-mile race.
With Sonny still keeping a chokehold on Rattler, we began ex-
amining him. Unfortunately, we decided, it was a pretty poor
specimen, at least by the standards of Uncle's story. It was not
near as big as the one Grandpa tamed, barely even half as big.

But this was *our how'ta*. We were going to tame it just the same
way Grandpa would have tamed it. Having forgotten our gunnysack, we had to take turns dragging the rattler by the head until
we got home. Mr. Rattler was probably very glad to get to our
home; at least he was no longer choked.

We put *how'ta* in a gunnysack, but decided it would be safer still if he were in the gunnysack in a hole in the ground with a big rock on top of it. We dug and dug. Soon we had a hole. We placed the rattler sack in there, then went in search of a flat rock or a heavy board to cover the hole. *How'ta* rested. He would need rest. In the morning we were going to tame him. We knew just how to do it, too.

We couldn't find a large flat rock or a large board, so we put some small boards over the hole and piled rocks on top to keep them in place. Then we got some fresh brush with leaves and piled it on top for camouflage. That ought to keep *how'ta* safe until tomorrow, and keep everybody away.

Next we picked the site for the taming on top of a little knoll near the house. *How'ta* would be at the highest point. We could run at him from any direction, kick him in the face or behind the head, and land on the other side, safe. It was perfect. We should have him tamed before breakfast.

I could not wait until tomorrow. The taming was all that I could think about. Yes, Grandpa would be proud. Maybe he will be in the trees, watching. Mom and Dad always say our ancestors are all around us all the time.

The window of the kids' bedroom had four sections. The bottom-left section had a corner broken out of it almost big enough to put my fist through. That night, through that little curved triangle I looked past the dirty window, past the stars and into a vastness, an expanse that was breathtaking. It was a wonderland that breathed in all directions. Then the stars and galaxies became stepping-stones to another vastness. It was fun jumping from star to star to galaxy and into another universe.

> *Grandpa was sitting in the fork of an oak tree, smiling as*
> *we tamed our first* how'ta. *We knew he was there because*
> *the leaves rustled in his tree when the rest of the forest was*

quiet. The taming took place in slow motion; sometimes everyone stood still for a long time, sometimes they moved very slowly.

Proud and determined, we drew straws to see who would go first. The longest straw got to be first. We each wanted the longest, to be the first to tame a rattler, just like Grandpa.

Because of our laws, Buddy, the youngest of the boys, didn't have to try to tame the rattler. He was three years old. There were three straws. I got the longest! I got to be first!

How'ta was coiled, and, like Uncle said, "cocked like a double-barreled shotgun." I ran and jumped over the snake, dragging my bare foot across his face, just for fun, like jumping from star to star. An oak tree trembled. I knew Grandpa was watching.

Sonny, then Kenny, kicked how'ta. How'ta *was tamed. The process was very easy. We dragged* how'ta *back to the lava beds and released him....*

BEFORE DAWN, as sun was fuzzing the horizon a silver-green, I woke up. We all did. In the early light we rushed to our den to see if *how'ta* was still there. He was still in the sack, which moved ever so slowly, rippling like soft thoughts or new ideas.

Soon it was light enough to see well. We rushed to the knoll, carrying *how'ta* in the sack. We put the sack in the open, and with Mr. Rattler still tied securely in the bag, we made some practice attempts. No matter what I thought about, when I got close to the sack, something between the pit of my stomach and my brain strained so badly that everything turned red trimmed with silver, and my belly froze. I was frightened witless, and the snake was still in the sack!

Meanwhile, I noticed that Kenny and Sonny were running at the sack, but at the last second they veered off to one side. They were afraid to jump over the sack, too!

The sun was filtering through the forest. If we were to tame *how'ta* before breakfast, we would have to move fast. Snake was still in the sack. Nobody had jumped over it yet.

With *how'ta* buzzing, rattling, and thrashing in anger, we finally untied the sack, caught the closed corners, and slowly poured him out into the light. He was mad! And somehow he had grown a couple of feet longer: His head was bigger, his tongue was longer, blacker, and whippier, and his rattles were immense!

Rattler's glassy eyes searched the landscape like a flashlight searching in the darkness. His gaze froze everybody. When he looked my way, something struck me in the pit of my stomach, knocking every ounce of wind out of me and causing that red glow trimmed with silver to flash across my consciousness.

My knees trembled and my spirit shook. This *how'ta* doctoring was a terribly frightening business. All of the trees in the forest rustled. I forgot about Grandpa. I wrenched my sight from the stare of *how'ta*.

It was now time to draw straws for real. Longest wins. One of us had to be sacrificed to the spirit of all snakes that morning, and I was very willing for it to be either Sonny or Kenny.

I closed my eyes as tight as I could, prayed, and drew. Oh no! I won!

I was going to embarrass all of the Snake Doctors in our history, I was going to embarrass myself, and I was going to die!

Since I had no shoes to take off, I was ready. I got dizzy again. In the back of my brain a red explosion was replaced by a black explosion, not pretty like the Fourth of July.

Sonny, Kenny, and Buddy were staring at me as if they meant to say good-bye. Then they focused on Rattler. They would live. I was sacrificed to the snake spirits. Relief was on their faces, fear glued, in gobs, upon my entire being.

Hoping to escape, I voted for a two-out-of-three drawing. They refused. I could not feel the rocks beneath my feet. I could barely hear and was having difficulty focusing.

This morning's session was not at all like my dream last night. In my dream I had floated over *how'ta* like a dandelion puffball and had even reached down and tapped Mr. Rattler on the nose. Now, coiled up over there, *how'ta* menaced me, seemingly ten feet high, arched, poised, mad, challenging, fearless, and hungry.

The entire forest was rippling. I studied the landscape for a while, then thought, "If my grandpa could do it, not only *can* I do it, but I will do it!"

Fortified by the thought that Grandpa was watching from every tree in the forest, I mentally prepared myself for the most dangerous leap of my entire seven-year-old life. But my imagination moved in and shoved my defense aside. Instead I saw a clear unveiling of my immediate future.

I LURCHED TOWARD HOW'TA. *My knees were wobbly, my legs weak, and I moved in slow motion. I closed my eyes and ran as hard as I could. But it was like racing away from fear in a nightmare; my legs would not move, but dragged behind. I was not nearing* how'ta *with enough speed to jump over him. Instead my body would collide terribly with the white, cold, poison-dripping fangs.*

How'ta *looked me straight in the eye. I was hypnotized, but somehow thought, "How did Grandpa do this the first time? We were told only about the last time!"*

I was nearing how'ta *very slowly. How'ta coiled, poised to strike deadly venom. Rattler had me timed: the closer I got, the farther back his head cocked. His mouth opened and two icy-looking, white needles pointed directly at the heart of my entire spirit. I could neither stop nor slow my already slow motion. Staring into the broken-glass mirror of how'ta's eyes, I came closer and closer, ever so slowly.*

I saw myself in the shine of his eyes, a shadowy outline. The long fangs, now unsheathed, were designed to thrust into the flesh and drive downward, pumping deadly poison in long spurts, like a dozen shots from the town doctor.

The fangs struck me on the top of the foot near the ankle. How'ta, *angrier than ever, writhed and twisted like a fish on a hook just out of the water, each movement causing the tips of the fangs to rip somewhere deep within me. Everything in my mind went red, then silver, then black.*

"COME ON, BOYS," Mom called. "Time to eat!"

We exploded homeward, leaving our fears and *how'ta* there on the Taming Knoll. My legs were working. I ran faster than I had ever run before, way ahead of the pack. The old house was approaching rapidly. But I ran clear past the house, clear past breakfast, and clear past the old, friendly barn.

I was alive and happy. It was so much fun being alive. I continued to run through the oak forest, then turned around and danced home. There was not much breakfast left, but I noticed the other boys were not wolfing their food. Today they took their time, eating slowly. Somehow it was very quiet. I ate the slowest of all.

Unable to wait any longer, we returned to the knoll. *How'ta* was gone. Of course we searched around for *how'ta*, but without much enthusiasm, finding only Uncle's empty green bottle where he had nestled it in the grass. We did a very poor job of pretending that we were surprised or disappointed that he was gone.

I saw some tracks in the morning dew. They were smaller than Daddy's and not store-bought shoes, but made from material that formed to the foot: *kla'klas* (moccasins)! I could see where the leaves were barely disturbed and found an occasional partial print in the vanishing dampness. The *kla'kla* tracks pointed toward the lava beds where we got *how'ta* in the first place.

I called the other boys, who shuffled over, thinking I had found *how'ta*, but before they got there, the tracks had vanished.

I peered into the morning forest. Over there on the point a lone tree rippled. I was sure Grandpa was proud of each of us.

Then I left the other boys and went into the solitude of the spring above the house. There I listened to the porcupines sing through their noses and the woodpeckers rattling on a dead snag, and again I heard in a whisper the voice of Mother calling us to breakfast, and, as the rest of the forest rippled, cried a deep and forlorn cry, so happy to still be alive.

CHAPTER SEVEN

SILVER BUBBLES

1946

We raced away from the house, carrying a rusty can half full of water and soap. We were going to make soap bubbles, and we wanted to do this without our sisters around. I was always happier away from my sisters because one of them always bothered me, always tried to treat me like I was her husband. I didn't like to look at them, and I didn't like to touch them, but most of all, I didn't like them to touch me. I ran every time, like Weasel evading Old Woman Frog.

In our narratives it is said that Frog chased Weasel clear to the moon. Moon tried to send Frog home, but she wouldn't go. She wanted Weasel. Moon told her to go away, that she was old and "looked pretty bad." She got mad, threatened Moon, and tried to swallow him, but she popped like bubble gum. Frog lost. It is said her skin is still stretched across the moon, those dark shadows that you can see best when the moon is full.

But today we were going to make magic. Soap bubbles always reminded me of shiny floating stars or silky moons close by. Stars and moons that we chased but we never caught. They always popped as soon as they touched our fingertips, or anything else.

Today was different. We were going to catch the shiny bubbles with our fingers, and they wouldn't pop because Daddy said if we got our hands wet with the same soapy water we were making bubbles with, we could catch the bubbles.

Several years ago our cousin showed us how to take a pine needle, curve it around, and shove the sharp end back into the pithy stem, making a circle. We made one and dipped it into the soapy water and tested it to make sure we could make a bubble—might need more soap. It worked! A shiny bubble!

Quickly we poured soapy water onto our hands and waited for the next bubble. It came, large and see-through shiny. Floating quietly, it moved away from us, and we quietly crept toward it, stretching out our sopping hands. We sneaked toward the bubble as if we were going to catch a butterfly resting in the sun.

Bubble dodged when a slight breeze caught it. We were nearer now and our excitement contained all of the enchantment of the mist created by the song of Silver-Gray Fox long ago. Like a part of our imagination, Bubble moved away and downward. We had to catch it before it hit something!

Wet little fingers reached toward the bubble. It shone and smiled, friendly. We touched the tiny silver beads on our sopping fingers, then reached out farther. Finally, two of us caught it. Stretching lazily, bubble balanced, but stayed on our fingers. We did it! We made magic—just like Silver-Gray Fox when he created the universe. Maybe we were just as good as Fox. Maybe we'll do more magic.

Bang! Down below the old barn there was a salt lick. Daddy must have spotted a deer there. We dropped our magic and ran past the barn, then dashed into the oak forest for a hundred yards. There Daddy crouched, the old .22 caliber rifle leaning against a tree. He was busy taking the guts out of a deer, a big, old doe.

Scars, maybe from barbed-wire snags, streaked her legs. "Mulie," Daddy said, a mule deer. I was hoping that this one couldn't have any more babies either.

"Go tell your mother to bring the truck."

The others raced toward the house. It didn't take everybody to get Mom, so I veered off into the old barn. It was sweet-sweaty-warm and sneezy with dust in there. But there were so many things to do, so many birds and insects to watch. Once in a while a rattler would buzz and shiver, then fold and withdraw under old boards and straw. Usually I had a warm feeling in that old barn, maybe because everything in there was mostly friendly.

After climbing high on the ladder nailed to one of the center posts of the barn, I could look down into the nests of pigeons and owls that were tucked in between the cedar-shake roof and the rafters. Fuzzy-topped baby birds watched the strange being climbing the ladder. Sometimes I couldn't see the birds because they huddled down until just their eyes were above the edge of the nest. Nobody could find me there; I was safe.

Soon the pickup rolled past the barn to get the deer. I waited.

Then the old truck puttered past the barn again toward home, and a few minutes later I smelled the liver and heart of the deer cooking in bacon grease. Mom always rolled them in flour, then dropped them into hot grease, cooking them quickly. I knew, too, that I had to get down from my barn hideaway and into the house before long, or all of the food would be gone. I always feared falling when coming down the ladder. I held my breath, leaning into the post with all my might, and moved as quickly as I could toward the floor.

I was too late. The meat was all gone before I got home. Daddy gave me some of his sandwich, deer liver wrapped in cold biscuit. It was good, crunchy, filling, salty, and satisfying. After eating I went out to the little ditch, lay on my belly, and drank from the clear, cold water. Little black bugs were darting beneath the leaves on the bottom, making "trails." The water was clean. The bugs must have been clean, too. Life just seemed to be clean and sweet.

I heard somebody coming. I did not look. Like Weasel in the old story, I ran, fleeing north on the old railroad tracks to the cave. A bear could be living in there now, but last time we'd been there it was empty—at least as far back as we could see. It would be a good hiding place.

Sneaking to the cave entrance, I heard only silence. I threw a rock in. It was dark and I could smell the dampness. Nothing stirred. I threw another rock. Nothing. I found a big stick and went in a little way. It was dank and quiet. I wondered if bats and owls lurked inside. My thoughts bounced back to me, an echo.

Watching carefully, I backed out of the cave and heard a rustling from somewhere in the nearby forest. Maybe it was a quail in the brush rattling the leaves, or maybe a squirrel, but the sound frightened me. I ran from the cave and on down the hill, making a big circle, and finally returned to the quiet safety of the barn, climbing high up, as far as I could go. In the silence and safety, I breathed more easily. Soon the barn life began moving. Buzzing. Chirping. Squirrels, pigeons, wasps, flies. Mice rustling in the hay far below.

A girl's shadow moved down the road from the house past the barn, moving like it was looking for something. I watched, holding my breath. The movement of the shadow disturbed all of the life in the privacy of the barn. In a little while the same shadow moved slowly back toward the house. My sister. I did not move. It took a long time for life to continue in the softness of the old barn.

It was just dark when Mom and Dad called for me. I lingered in the black shadows of the barn in the blue of evening. It was time to wash up and get ready for bed. But I did not like sleeping in the same room—especially not with my sisters. More quiet than a mouse, I crept into bed. The stars slipped secretly by.

I was hardly ever sleepy after being chased, so I lay there in the bedroom in the darkness and daydreamed. In the distance, through the broken corner window of the room, I could see clouds. The clouds turned into mist, and my spirit began a journey on that swirl into a time long ago.

CHAPTER EIGHT

THE MORNING THE SUN WENT DOWN FOREVER

1947

Fate is, at times, like love. It can be beautiful. It can be tragic. In the days of my youth, a day's labor for a Native American man could not produce enough money to purchase the necessary supplies to feed a family of eight children and two adults. Money was scarce since Daddy had been unemployed for a long time. As a consequence, food and necessities were scarce, too. The whole world seemed to be throw-up disgusting.

On this day my mother and father, with my baby brother and the two youngest of the family, were returning home from a trip to town with whatever they could purchase. The older five children were in school. I was in the second grade. We all knew that there was not enough money for our needs. We wore ragged clothes and went barefoot most of the time, summer and winter.

After buying the absolute necessities in Fall River Mills, Mom and Dad discovered that they had no money for gasoline. Daddy hoped he could reach home on the gas in the tank. Normally, it was a journey of eighteen miles if we followed the oiled road, but Daddy knew a shortcut. Still, they ran out of gas when they were almost home.

The dirt road that turned from Highway 89 to the Old Home Place was on the east side of Lake Britton Bridge. Approaching the bridge on both sides were long and steep grades of about a mile each. Below the bridge, muddy Lake Britton. The entire countryside is an immense chalk deposit, diatomaceous, the scientists would say. The bridge is in the center of a huge U-turn.

Loaded trucks, coming from Burney, usually gain speed from the downhill grade approaching the bridge in order to climb the opposite grade more easily. With their engines wound up, running at full bore, they can "walk" up the other side. The road is constructed in such a manner that a trucker can see another vehicle approaching from the Mount Shasta direction and make adjustments.

The gasoline gauge registered "empty" for some time, my father told me later, and just before our turnoff, a hundred feet beyond Lake Britton Bridge, the engine popped, sputtered, then quit. Daddy managed to maneuver the automobile until it was almost off the left side of the highway, just entering the road to the Old Home Place. Traffic coming from Burney should be in the lane that Daddy had just left, and traffic coming from Mount Shasta would see the vehicle in plenty of time to slow down and pass without incident.

The noon sun was warming the autumn earth. The pavement was dry, and the first storms had not yet come.

After uttering a good many oaths about the world situation and the empty gas tank, Daddy told Mom to stay in the car with Baby Jerry and told Buddy and Fefe to go play nearby. He got out and attempted to push the car the rest of the way off the highway and into our driveway. Mom jumped out to help. The car would not budge.

Daddy said the baby started to cry, left alone for a few minutes.

Mother quickly returned to him. He persisted in screaming, although Mother spoke softly to him, saying "baby" several times as she bounced him on her lap. For some reason, our baby brother was scared.

Daddy could hear the high-pitched scream that indicated a speeding truck. He recognized this sound from the time he had been employed as a truck driver for the meat packing company in Fall River Mills.

A white chalk bank was between the car and the oncoming truck and the bank was just high enough to obstruct the view of traffic approaching from the bridge. In an attempt to signal the oncoming truck that it should stay in the right-hand lane, Daddy raced for the bridge.

The huge vehicle, loaded with lumber, hurtled at an alarming speed across the bridge, shaking and rattling the structure. It was in the wrong lane and seemed out of control. Daddy's instincts screamed "DANGER!" The grinding rumble of the truck and its frightening thunder as it screamed across the silver bridge warned Daddy to get his family out of the car.

The truck had nearly fifty yards of bridge to cover in the time it took the man to cover fifty feet. It was bellowing now like a mad bull. It passed so close he could touch it. The trucker was familiar with this stretch of the road, for he was getting a "jump" on the long climb. To climb the opposite grade more easily, the trucker chose to take the inside lane, putting his deadly weapon directly into line with our auto, the singing mother, and her baby. If he saw Daddy he probably just thought that a crazy Indian was waving to him. Black smoke belched upward from twin stacks mounted high on the cab.

Daddy heard the engine take a deep gulp as fuel and air were forced into its combustion chambers. Chains rattling, it roared toward the rapidly approaching incline. On foot, he raced toward his little family. He could just see Mom now, sitting in the front seat, holding Baby. "Get out! Get out!" he screamed. "Run!"

"God, Good Goddamned God, NO!"

The truck had already flashed past him. Its redheaded driver did not see the car until the nose of his truck was lined up directly with the rear end of the auto, only a half a moment away. At that speed, he could not turn the wheels. With a full load of lumber, he could not stop. The tires made deep black marks on the pavement as they desperately tried to obey the air brakes, tires screaming like a perishing dinosaur. Now Daddy could hear the gulp of the engine again, as if the truck itself had seen the car and ceased to breathe.

From this moment on, his eyes were filled with disbelief and terrible pain. I did not see those eyes at that instant. I saw them later. That was enough. A prayer, hope, and love were all shattered in the moment it takes to gasp a single breath.

Out of the corner of her eye, Mother saw a huge blur approaching. She threw open the door of the automobile and took a few steps. The baby was clutched to her breast.

The driver of the truck was frozen to the wheel. Even with the brake pedal slammed to the floor, the hot tires screaming and smoking, the truck failed to slow. It continued in an unwavering direction toward the stalled car. It was as though the driver was on a seek-and-destroy mission. His weapon: the truck. His objective: the automobile, the frightened mother, and little baby. Mission: accomplished.

The truck struck the black automobile a horrendous blow, knocking it off the ground and smashing it against the side of the chalk bank. The automobile exploded. The cab of the truck bounced across the highway, where it came to a stop in the ditch with its left wheels spinning in the chalk-dusty atmosphere of death and shattered dreams.

The chains binding the load snapped. Tons of lumber pummeled the auto, the earth, and the doomed mother and child. Whether she screamed or not, Daddy could not tell. He was now suspended somewhere in an unreal world. He did not believe what he saw. He could not believe it. This could not be happening. His wife and child could not be under that huge pile of lumber.

"This can't happen! You're asleep, Herman. Wake up! Wake up!" his mind screamed. At that same instant, three people met death, but in a different manner. His wife and infant son died instantly. He died over and over, again and again.

Insane beyond fear, he ran to the huge, jumbled pile of timbers. The air was filled with dust, with death. He sensed it. His nostrils smelled the fresh blood, and his stomach grew weak and slick. Yet he grabbed the timbers that covered his wife and child and threw them violently from the pile.

He tried to dig through the tons of lumber to reach them. He moved as if in a dream of underwater slowness, pushing, pulling, and bullying the timbers. Suddenly, a loosened pile crashed down on him, almost breaking his leg. He yanked his leg free and again, like an attacking bulldog, tore away at the lumber pile. It was his enemy.

Daddy did not notice that several cars had stopped, that people were helping him. He did not see the trucker climb dirty, bloody, and frightened, from the cab of his truck and run to where he desperately labored. Daddy only noticed the trucker when he started tearing at the pile along with him. They now worked as a slow-motion team.

Daddy knew deep inside that it was futile. He would have vomited had he not been so filled with desperation. Soon, many people were helping. Faster! Faster! Throw off the timbers. The pile diminished, but not fast enough. Faster!

Then he saw a black jacket and a plastic flower pinned to it, the flower he had bought long ago. Inside the jacket, his wife. Dark blood stained the lumber. Some dropped from the end of a board. It was warm and moved like red honey, slick. He touched it and did not understand. The blood on his fingers felt like two pieces of silk brushed lightly together. Quickly! Remove the rest of the lumber. Hurry! Then, there she lay in the bright sunlight. The breath of life crushed from her.

Daddy could not move, only stare with empty eyes. She was carefully lifted by some unknown persons and laid on the timbers. Under her was the baby. After the lumber was removed, the mother and baby's faces that had been instantly flattened now somehow took on their former images.

Blood covered the ground and soaked the clothes of the mother and child. Under her head, a pool of red, crushed from her lungs, bright and bubbly. The blood was dark, almost black, some already clotted in lumps, like small livers. My father smelled the blood and the dust mingled with the odor of burning rubber from the truck tires sliding hard upon the pavement. He did not feel his hands, tired and torn.

A small, bright-red spot indicated where the baby's lungs had exploded only a second before his mother's. Their blood had been the same only months earlier, he still in her womb, in life. Now it mixed again, in death.

Daddy, exhausted and beaten, fell down on the bloodstained timbers and gathered his wife and son into his trembling arms. There he remained for a long time. Not crying. Not praying. Not living. Then he cried, his tears mingling with the red earth. His body shook, but he did not make another sound. There was none in him.

Eventually, medical assistance came; from where he did not know. He was thinking about the song he always sang to Mom,

> You are my sunshine, my only sunshine.
> You make me happy when skies are gray.
> You do not know dear, how much I love you,
> So please don't take my sunshine away.

Now, as a stretcher was lain down beside him, he slowly let his wife and baby son go. A vast amount of sunshine abandoned him.

Buddy and Fefe watched this event from beside the railroad tracks where they had been playing. A vast amount of sunshine abandoned them, too. They still tremble when I ask them about it. Fragments of a shattered puzzle are yet within them. Sometimes, painfully, they speak about it. They went to Daddy and touched him. He did not feel them. They were frightened. They too were alone. Aloneness came to be our ever-present companion.

NOW I KNOW WHY Daddy often muttered in anger: "God damn you, God! God damn you!" In lonesome pain, bewildered and lost, Daddy now felt that he had nothing, and that life had no meaning or purpose. He could not accept the responsibility of caring for the family that was left him by the tragedy. But there were children, eight to be exact, each with a lot less "sunshine." Confused and lost, he started on a long, painful, and crooked path through life, turning away from his family, his spirit damaged beyond repair.

His eyes were empty of sparkle. He looked long at objects without seeing them—and often the other children and I were the objects. He was a man without a reason to live. Now his shelter from the life-raping storms of loneliness was alcohol. He forced himself to it. Any kind. Any place. With anybody. Or alone.

They were buried in the same casket, the child sleeping at her breast. They were real-looking to my seven-year-old eyes, but cold and unmoving. I kissed them both. It was like kissing wood. Flowers were piled high upon the casket and upon the grave. But they were of no use now. Why didn't they bring flowers when Mama and Jerry were alive?

At the graveside, surrounded by a throng of wailing fat and skinny women and men of all shapes and ages, my father was alone. Oblivious to almost everything, he watched them bury his wife and child. From the first shovel of dirt, his heart was as much buried as were his wife and child. Many times he came to that spot and stood under the pine trees and simply stared at the grave. Staring, refusing to believe.

From then on Daddy lived in a world of shadows. He was injured when the lumber crashed down upon him, a grim reminder of the accident. And his heart was critically wounded now. He lived in a constant panic, like a deer that has been shot through the heart, yet continues to flee from danger, not knowing that its destination has already been decided.

I went with Daddy once. Only when he went to her grave could he gather parts of himself that were yet a man. Holding his tear-stained face to the sky and the seasons where he was certain her spirit now dwelled, he spoke her name, "Laura, my Laura. Come back. Please...." Then, and only then, he felt that he was not completely dead.

For the remainder of his life, a moment did not pass when he did not think of that little grave in the Old Home Place cemetery. In his sleep he relived the footrace with that huge machine. In a quiet moment he said he constantly heard the truck rush past him. While awake he heard the impact and saw the truck twist and mangle the car. He saw the lumber, in slow motion, pile over his wife and child. At this memory, he physically winced. That is why people thought he was "punchy." It hurt. It hurt!

There was no cure in this world for his pain. Not prayer. Not alcohol. Not God. Not another woman. Nothing. Yes, death might be a most pleasant journey compared to the path he was now wandering.

One day the state of California (our constant enemy) came and took us away from Daddy. They said they were taking us to a place where we could go to school, and somebody would take care of us. It is true, Daddy neglected us. It is true that he was incapacitated. It is true that alcohol and his "friends" combined to make his life more miserable. He took the little rifle and shot at us one day as we ran through the brush, fleeing for our lives. Soon the state captured us.

Daddy was my first teacher. He taught me about making an *arrangement* with the deer instead of hunting it, about the proper bait to use for each variety of fish in the streams and in the lake, about fixing automobiles, about boxing. He showed me how to call a rabbit with the whistling of a reed held between the index fingers and the thumbs, and he taught me about an awesome power that surrounds all of life, from the heart of the earth to the ends of the vastness of the universe.

He was my father but I cannot remember if I ever told him how much I loved him. How much I needed him. How much the family needed him now more than ever.

I refused for years to learn anything in the white-man way. The white man represented "invasion" to me. The state has always been the "they" in my life, the enemy. Captured, I constantly compared the lessons of nature that Daddy taught me with the lessons that the Americans forced upon me through their foreign rules. And the lessons of the Americans pale.

Daddy's spirit surrendered one day. That awesome power that holds the entire universe failed him. Drunk, they said. Fifteen years after the morning the sun went down forever, we buried Daddy next to Mom and Jerry.

CHAPTER NINE

WA-LOW-CHAH

⬥

1947

All the world was shadows moving among shadows, or shadows standing in front or in back of each other, peering, whispering. The sounds of human life often made my stomach churn, as if I had just eaten a heaping spoonful of rancid mayonnaise. I wandered around, usually by myself. Life drained of beauty. I cried in silence and in shame of being alone. All alone.

I ached very deeply, an ache that refused to go away. I hurt mostly when I remembered being told that Mom and Baby Jerry died instantly, that they had felt no pain. No pain? How could anybody alive know if there was pain or not? How many of them had been killed, crushed by a lumber truck? How many of them had just died? How could they know there was no pain? If Mom and Jerry had felt no pain, why did the rest of the family suffer so much sorrow?

At seven years old, my life withered and turned a silent gray, like an old-time photograph of Indians in feathers and Buffalo Bill in buckskin. A photograph curled up at the edges, sun-cracked and moisture-warped. I had to escape. So, as the Elders of my tribe advised, "Just dream." I dreamed, and I heard an old, deep voice telling about how the *Qwillas* (giant lizards

79

the size of dinosaurs) were run out of *Latowni* (Pitville ceremonial lodge) long ago.

No. That is a lesson of conflict, of war, pain, and destruction. I did not want to dream about that. I switched dreams. I heard a voice whispering in the distance, difficult to measure, a voice unsure of the American language, telling about Cloud Maiden. It wasn't Grandpa's voice; it was older, shakier, earthier—one of the Keepers of our Narratives.

> "Kwaw, *Silver Fox Man, see cloud north. He want know. Silver Fox get name, dream. Dream give him* Annikadel. Annikadel *wise, help make world.* Kwaw *dream four clouds come, each way. North cloud, Cloud Maiden, girl in there.*"

> *Kwaw*, who is Silver Fox Man and one of the makers of the world, saw a cloud in the north. He wanted to know what it was. Silver Fox dreamed and his dream brought him *Annikadel*, a powerful spirit who also helped create the world. *Annikadel* was the wisest of all beings who, after helping make the world as it is today, turned into the blue-bellied lizard. Silver Fox had a dream that four clouds came, one from each direction. The cloud from the north contained a girl, Cloud Maiden.

> "*Morning*, Kwaw *look north. North cloud cover sky.* Kwaw *think rain. He watch. He sleep, dream. Dream spoke, 'When you awake, girl will singing.'* Annikadel *made tree for eagle. Dream spoke, 'Sweet water spring near tree. Basket, cup each* tosaq-jami ajoq je-he' [*The design on the cup and the basket are beautiful*]. *Dream spoke, 'Give water, girl. She travel far.' He get magic cup, get water magic basket live beside magic tree, gave girl.*"

In the morning Silver Fox awoke and looked north. He saw clouds covering the sky. He thought it was going to rain, so he slept and dreamed again. His dream told him that when he woke up, a woman would be singing.

Annikadel, because of his wisdom, made the first tree. He prepared it for a future event. He made the tree with his thought and with his magic power. Silver Fox's dream told him that a sweet-water spring lived near a tree, along with a basket and a cup, and that each had beautiful designs on them. The dream told Silver Fox to give Cloud Maiden a drink because she had traveled far and was thirsty. Silver Fox obeyed the instructions given in his dream and gave Cloud Maiden a drink of sweet water from the spring, using the beautiful basket and beautiful cup.

"Kwaw *like girl. Ask live him be sister* [*wife*]. *She spoke: 'Can't. Come sky. Not live earth. Born in air.'* Kwaw *sleep.* Wa-low-chah *go back air.* Kwaw, *Cloud Maiden nice.*"

Silver Fox fell in love with Cloud Maiden and asked her to live with him and be his wife. This was so long ago there were not yet relations, so *Kwaw* called her "sister." She could not accept his offer, stating that she came from the sky and was not designed to live on earth. While Silver Fox was sleeping, Cloud Maiden went back to the sky. Silver Fox dreamed nice dreams about Cloud Maiden.

"Annikadel *see.* Wa-low-chah *he change* Lo'we'chah, *Eagle Woman. They live* Ticado Hedache."

Annikadel saw that Silver Fox and Cloud Maiden loved each other and wanted to live together, so he turned Cloud Maiden into Eagle Woman. She came and lived on earth with Silver Fox, resting in the tree that *Annikadel* had prepared at the heart of the world for this occasion. As *Lo'we'chah*, she could still return to the sky at will. They loved each other, it is said, forever. And the Keepers of the Narratives still say that the tree, the basket, the spring, and the cup can be seen there at *Ticado Hedache*, the heart of the world.

FROM DREAM TO CLOUD to eagle to beautiful woman, with love. From loneliness to happiness, filled with magic, and living in the heart of the world. Yes, that is the story I wanted to listen to with my spirit.

And later, during the transformation, they say *Annikadel* turned into the blue-bellied lizard. In the summer, lizards did "push ups" just before we chased them under the rocks and through the rustling leaves.

Wandering nowhere, I thought about the Cloud Maiden; then I heard singing to the west. I listened for a long time, not breathing, not hearing anything. Again. There it was, in the softly shifting winds in the forest and the canyon: Mom!

Softly and far, far away, she was singing to my baby brother, Jerry. I trembled. Then I ran. Across the valley, through the brush, up the mountainside, over rocks. Torn and exhausted after running blindly, I lay under the oaks, looking through the leaves and watching clouds float slowly by.

Why couldn't I be a cloud and go away to where Mom and Jerry were? I didn't seem to matter, anyway. My life was a vacuum. Like the medicine powers that abandoned Uncle Ramsey, long ago. He said he could not be a medicine man because the powers left him. They traveled west, down the canyon and over the mountains. I could float west, too, through the great canyon, over the mountains and away, maybe even past the great salt sea.

Mother sang, and her voice came from all directions. Then my baby brother Jerry cried from somewhere. I shuddered because I could not follow them, not in all directions.

IMMEDIATELY AFTER Mom's death, her mother (owning a greater share of the property according to the legal papers made in the Bureau of Indian Affairs office in Sacramento) began a campaign for us to move away so she could sell the land. She wanted money. She was full-blood *Iss,* but she was married to an Italian white man, and they both wanted money. They cared little if we children had a place to live. And Gram, very dark complexioned herself, hated Daddy, always referring to him as "that black man." So, after Mom's death, when the state of California took us away from Daddy, we began our crooked trail of broken foster homes. Quickly we became landless people.

At their burial, some people had cried because they cared for Mom and for Baby Jerry, and were truly sorry for their deaths. But some came to mock. Old and ugly tribal hatreds still smoldering, leaping to flames in one generation, then smoldering again in the next. The emotion of hate has always fractured my people. Like broken obsidian, it cannot be healed, and often hate has no more of a foundation than rumor.

I looked upon those mocking faces, and my spirit turned hard like winter stone. They were of the same families that always wanted to sell our homeland to the Americans. Their vanity, inflated by the Americans praising them with hollow words, always caused them to be contrary to the best wishes of the tribe.

I wished that they would die. They did not. I was too small to attack and kill them, but I wanted to. Then in a pact with and a demand upon my spirit, I vowed that the mockers would never grin, looking upon me in a grave. I decided at that moment to live longer than them all.

CHAPTER TEN

IT'AJUMA

1947

"There they are!" Sonny hollered, pointing from our "lookout" on top of the chalk bank on the school side of Lake Britton Bridge. We had left school at lunch time and were waiting to meet Daddy, Buddy, and Fefe halfway between home and the school. Our eyes searched across Lake Britton Bridge and east up the old railroad track looking for any movement. We used that old, abandoned railroad track to walk to school and home again. They came slowly moving toward us—Daddy and the youngest two children, Buddy and Fefe. Mom and Baby Jerry had just been buried, and Daddy was drinking wine more and more with people who could not possibly be his friends, nor ours.

They were carrying a paper sack. In that sack, our lunch. Having no breakfast and walking to school and back as far as the bridge, I was hungry. Our lunch was usually homemade bread with peanut butter and jelly, or some type of dried meat.

WE ARE A FISHING, hunting, gathering culture. In the old days nature simply fed us. Before Pacific Gas and Electric Company began placing dams across the Sacramento River down in the val-

ley and on the Pit River in the mountains, our people had fished
for salmon and sea-run trout. After the dams were put across the
river to create electricity, the salmon and other ocean-run fish
were denied access to our homeland. Almost half of our diet was
barred from our tribal lands.

Once Daddy and I were out fixing fence for the Kaupangers.
We rode our grass-sweet-smelling horses, Cap and Fox, to work,
getting there very early. The Kaupangers, a German family, lived
nearby. Daddy and I had worked for them off and on while we
were preparing the old home place for our own family just the
summer before.

I was so very hungry since we had not had any time to fix
breakfast. Besides, making a few dollars was more important than
eating at that time. We needed nails more than we needed food.
Daddy told me about an old-timer who was so hungry he could
eat the south end of a skunk traveling north. Boy, I was hungri-
er'n that today.

Daddy thought that we could finish the fence before noon, or
at least before we got so hungry that we began "eatin' barb wire."
I almost tried the barbed wire but any thought of eating made my
stomach growl and my whole head have a toothache.

Just a piece of *wa'hach*. Maybe some pine nut seeds. Anything,
even dirt! I began looking for *ap'as* (small sweet roots that we
gather in the spring) instead of helping Daddy. "Wrong time of
year, son. Too late."

Just then, Mrs. Kaupanger appeared and floated across the
field, dress fluttering in the breeze, carrying a plate covered with
waxed paper. She also had a small container of lemonade. And
she smiled. Still, I kept Daddy between her and me.

I smelled something! It was "something," but I had no idea
what. The fragrance exploded from whatever was on that plate

under that waxed paper. It made me dizzy. My knees trembled. I sat down in the dirt to keep them from buckling. What an aroma! After talking for what seemed to be a hundred long years, Daddy handed me a white-man's sandwich. My first taste of tuna fish. Oh, my!

Nothing on earth has ever matched that delicate flavor. The tuna was lightly salted, sprinkled with black pepper, and spread upon fresh, home-baked bread. It had a leaf of lettuce, and it was mixed with an amazing invention, mayonnaise.

That sandwich was a miracle made tasty. It petted my spirit while it fed my quaking body. It quieted the famished multitude of snakes writhing inside my belly. Amazing. There must have been a sliver of onion somewhere within that mixture of flavors: far in back my nose I detected a faint onion flower, a blossom freshness that still lingers within the recess of my memory. A flavor, an aroma, never equaled. My spirit has been searching for that exact flavor ever since.

At that moment, my spirit was so happy it cried. Then it giggled. That evasive tuna flavor, that festive bouquet, the taste of that lunch was chiseled upon the granite of my consciousness.

I KNEW FOR SURE there was not going to be a tuna fish sandwich in the sack that Buddy and Fefe took turns carrying toward us on the old railroad tracks. We famished children watched them approach, like crows waiting in a tree. After we wolfed our lunch, Daddy, Buddy, and Fefe turned homeward, and we returned to school.

Often it was a pleasant walk to school, but school itself was a terrible ordeal, and I hated every moment of it. I was doing very badly in my studies, and I did not want to enter the classroom, but I did not want to go home either because the possibility of disaster lurked everywhere. Daddy had no job. We lived near the grave of Mom and Jerry. There seemed to be no future for any of us. Poverty was our constant companion. Happiness deserted me. My life seemed to be falling apart, and education wasn't saving me.

English—a very strange and crooked language, in volumes too many to count. Writing—a distortion of my fingers and an invasion of my dreams. History—a study of a series of events that blurred and ruined parts of every day. The only thing worse than history was mathematics—a headache of uncontrollable scratches that constantly moved upon the paper and meant something different with each movement. Mathematics attacked my mind with invisible bullets. My spirit screamed and fled into the dark recesses of my mind's caverns, but that didn't seem to help.

Sometimes I could not sleep, trying to get the figures of mathematics straight in my thinking. I would stack the numbers, but they always fell over into a mess. I would stack them again, but they would fall again, now the other way, into a bigger mess. When the numbers turned into crawling worms, I gave up and slept a fitful sleep, dreading the morning, when I would have to enter the schoolhouse door again.

I cannot remember many of my teachers, except Mrs. Hewitt, a white woman who had a daughter named Gail. I remember Gail because we were not enemies; she did not wear that "untouchable" aura around her. I never talked to her, only glanced in her direction. I felt no threat coming from her, as it came from almost all the other white people I had met. She did not "accuse" me with her eyes or attitude. It seemed that she simply was there, and I simply was there, too. When Gail was absent from school, my life hurt a little bit for an unknown reason.

The school house was small and white. In a clearing out back among the trees, we played kickball, though I could not understand the game and did not have much fun. At least running was fun and sure beat sitting in the school house, wondering what I was doing there. I should have been home hunting with Daddy. Maybe some of his pain from Mom's death would go away, and he could get a job, and we could move, and we would have a better life, somewhere, somehow, some way.

When we were in class, I scrunched down in the seat as far as I could so the teacher would not ask me a question about history or make me go to the blackboard and do a math problem. I thought that if she could not see me, she would not call my name. Whenever she did call on me, a red-yellow blob splashed across my consciousness, like somebody had hit me hard in the brain with a baseball bat. Mrs. Hewitt must have known I was in total agony.

Another problem I had was saluting the flag. It took me a long time to learn how. Nobody ever explained why this activity was necessary or what it meant.

It was terrible to be dumb! In class, everything I read or heard always went blank. Somehow it just would not "stick." The blackboard of my mind was blank. It frightened me to wonder why my brain remained that way.

If I was doomed to dumbness forever, why not stay home and go hunting with Daddy? Now that was a great idea. Or we could go fishing in Lake Britton. Maybe we could go visit somebody who was not drinking wine. Tokay, Port, Muscatel. They all smelled bad, like something rotting.

Fishing, that's it. We could go down to the river. Just last year Daddy and I walked along the Pit River. He stopped and looked high up into the trees. There, nestled against the bark and resting among the limbs and shadows of a huge oak tree was a long-handled spear. It did not have one of the old, traditional spear heads for salmon, rather a metal one, welded together. It was square, with four widely spaced tines. This spear was made for sucker fish.

Once, after a long wait, my patience expired, and Daddy made me go away from the shallows and sit on the bank at a little distance. When the water moiled right beside him, he drove the spear into the water, holding whatever it was that he had speared to the bottom of the river until its struggling ceased and his spear stopped dancing. Then he reached down with one hand and grabbed the huge sucker fish by the gills. With the spear still run through it, and Daddy's thick fingers in its gills, the fish could not possibly escape. We ate for two days on that big fish, but it had a million bones!

Later, when Daddy and I were "opening" the Old Home Place, we went to the river. He said we were going fishing, but we took no hook and line. We could always find something to use for a fishing pole, but this day we did not take any tackle. I wondered but stumbled along as best I could while still watching for grasshoppers for bait.

The river seemed placid, hissing over the ripples heading toward the ocean. It was clear and clean. Three *et'wi* (eagles) were sitting in a tree where the morning angle of the sun allowed them a perfect view of the river bottom. From their perch they could clearly see all of the life moving there, the fish swimming about. They waited for the ospreys to swoop down and snag a trout or sucker. Then the eagles would attack the osprey in the air, a dog fight. Often the osprey would drop their prey, and an eagle would fold and dive, streaking to catch the silver fish in midair. The birds performed a beautiful sky ballet. When the eagles were gathered and waiting, we knew fish were feeding nearby.

We walked carefully along the river to a deep pool. Daddy reached far down into the water and began tugging on something. I thought it was a root of a tree, but in a few moments he withdrew a trout spear. It was longer than the sucker spear, and whippier. Daddy said he had to pierce the trout in the head with the spear in order to catch it properly. This late in the morning, trout stayed in deeper water than the suckers, so he could not reach down and catch them by the gills once he speared them. The spear head was much smaller than the one we used for suckers. Its three tines were almost fragile in comparison to the huge ones on the sucker spear.

We studied the eagles who were surveying the river bottom, and located their angle to the sun. Since trout spook so very easily, and vanish quicker than a thought, Daddy made me sit far back in the shadows. He took the long-handled spear and fed it into the water, easing it so slowly. Then he waited. I do not know how Daddy could wait so long without moving, without breathing.

Eagles watched, I watched, sun watched, and Daddy waited, studying, and becoming a part of all the activity along the river.

Though I was watching, I did not see his lightning thrust. In an instant a silver flash thrashed at the end of the spear far down in the water. Soon Daddy was fighting the trout out of the deep water, steering it into the shallows and eventually onto the bank. The spear handle vibrated as the trout frantically tried to free itself. But big rainbow was doomed to become our dinner.

The fish, fat and silver, had a bright pink stripe running from its gills almost to the tail. It was beautiful, but its eyes showed the unknown pain of death.

The *et'wi* looked at each other almost in disbelief that Daddy and I would come to *their* river and steal *their* trout. They stretched their huge wings, adjusted their claws upon the limbs, then peered down the river, looking for the silver-white flash of a fishing osprey.

Daddy replaced the spear in the deep water of the river under

the roots and rocks. As we carried the huge silver trout homeward, he explained that anybody in the family who was supposed
to knows where the spears are. They belonged to the whole tribe
and anyone could use them if they had learned not to abuse the
privilege of fishing, nor to abuse the responsibility of being
human in the conduct of life's balance with death.

CHAPTER ELEVEN

GOOSE VALLEY

❦

1947

Not long after the burial of Mom and Jerry, when I was seven years old, we were in court in Redding, California. The judge ordered us kids to "approach the bench." We did not know what bench he was talking about. There were benches out in the hall, outside on the grass, in the park beneath the railroad overpass where the winos gathered, and one near the woman in the court who was writing down every question and response. Which bench?

The sheriff shuffled us around with his hands, paper-white on top and thick pink on the palms. Soon we were standing awkwardly before Judge Richard B. Eaton. He was a small man with a black mustache, gray eyes, and those clean, powdery, white hands, vivid against the intense black of his robe. He explained that we were now under the custody of the State of California, and that we must obey his laws because he was the one from now on who was responsible for each of us. I did not understand. The massive, white sheriff standing so close scared me. He was like a horse with a saddle on it, huge, sweaty, and smelling of leather. I could not hear a word. Everything blurred and vanished into a bleakness. All I knew was that I had no Mom, and Dad was drunk, somewhere.

With the banging of his gavel upon the wooden anvil, we children, the remnants of our frightened little family, were now relocatable property of the State of California, no voice dissenting. It was like being a dog or a horse, a possession. Not like a cat. Nobody owns a cat. Nobody can tell cats what to do, have them sit up, or roll over. Yes, it was like being a dog. A dog in the dust with four broken legs, so scared it can't even whimper.

The Redding Court House was gray outside. Inside it was thick with moving shadows, and the whole building smelled lonesome. I thought being inside the building was like being in a place where dead people were operated on, or where everybody was sick and preparing to die. And it was frightening. Everything black-gray, hollow eyes peering here and there, or nowhere at all. Black shoes, black dresses; gray suits, gray dresses. No smiles. Stern faces in a panic, scurrying in many directions. The state employees seemed to have no destination, but were in a hurry to get there. Waving a piece of paper in their hand, they did not mind shoving us kids out of their way. *Merkans!* (Americans) Daddy's great-aunt would hiss.

The sheriff's hair was gray, his skin light gray, his clothes pale gray. His billy club was black, as were his handcuffs. But the pistol he wore at his waist shone like his star-shaped badge, and the copper bullets seemed to be in a happy row along his belt.

The judge spoke a very strange English; at least it was strange compared to the English I had heard in first and second grade.

I didn't understand, neither in that moment nor for many years. Somebody later explained that a judge often speaks Latin. However, at such an early age, I reasoned that Latin was a form of Greek, which, in turn, was another form of English, but spoken beyond the eastern ocean in a funny way. I began to worry if the judge was telling the truth in this other English language, or if he was saying something I did not understand, which would harm me before long.

The language coming from that gray and shadowy courthouse imposed itself upon me and seemed to threaten my life. It attached itself to the back of my neck and somehow clung to my earlobes. If I turned my head quickly, it seemed to stretch like a spider's web, then retract when I turned my head straight.

We four boys and four girls were legally assigned to live with Raymond (a white man) and Reitha Amen (granddaughter of Sampson Grant, a leader of our people who was born in Hat Creek around 1850 and died in Goose Valley in 1940), friends of the family. At that time they lived in Burney, but we had to move to Goose Valley, to Sampson Grant's homestead, where there was more land and a larger house. Living with our own people and out in the wilds of nature was a relief, and since Reitha was from our tribe, we managed to survive a little better.

However, during the lonely and painful days and nights, there was no one who knew my feelings. Daddy had always come the closest, but after that, nobody. I was never close to any of my sisters because I never had fun with them. After Mother's death, the girls became total strangers to me, biologically connected through our mother and our father and our ancestors, but so distant they could have come from beyond the moon.

Hurting, with no one to talk to, I heeded the advice of the old people, I dreamed.

IN OUR OLD BLACK CAR, the family bounced along an old road. We were going to a place called Dixie Valley, past Bob's Creek, where Uncle Ramsey was born so long ago it was hard for the mountains to remember. Our car was full of kids all jumping around, making excited noises with Mom and Dad and Baby Jerry in the front. Once in a while Daddy would roar over the front seat like *wer'ak'mita* (mountain lion), and we would settle down for a few miles. Then we would begin again until the next roar.

We crossed a pretty little bridge over Dixie Creek, past flowers waving to us and birds seeming to sing a welcome song. We came out of the forest with its flickering shadows and into a wide valley lit by early spring sunshine. The creek, with tall white flowers standing sentinel beside it here and there, ambled over near the edge of the valley where the forest abruptly stopped, but it seemed to want to march on into the meadow.

Lo'we'chah (Eagle Woman) circled high in the soft blue, then folded and darted northwest toward the great canyon. A family of deer jumped the rail fence one after the other (the spotted fawns crawled under the wire) and disappeared into the shadows of the trees. A marmot whistled, sounding like my brother imitating birds and animals in the forest. Meadowlarks sang over the flowers and little birds shuffled, often upside down, around the stems of the taller flowers and the willows.

We rambled into the old yard, dust curling heavily behind us. Several very old people were outside on a broken-down porch attached to an old crooked house with smoke coming straight up out of the chimney, blue smoke from juniper wood. It has a sweet, welcome-home aroma, juniper. Some of the windows of the aged building were broken and covered with boards. A gathering of people scattered near the porch was listening to an ancient person speaking a narrative.

The other kids all scattered like quail in every direction. But I went to the crooked porch with Mom and Dad. There was a slight break in the "talk," with welcomes and warm smiles from dark faces with black-brown eyes, shiny eyes. An Elder, white hair tied back in a bun behind his head, offered us water. We drank deeply like weary travelers, took a long breath, then joined in the listening. The Elder continued his "talk."

"Qwilla *he eat people every time. He,* Qwilla, *kill it, take home. Get home they ate* Latowni *people, people live* chema-ha."

Qwillas are large lizard-like dinosaurs and they killed the *Iss/Aw'te* people and took them home and ate them. The people they preyed upon lived in a ceremonial house (*chema-ha*) at *Latowni,* now the town of Pittville, California.

"He come again. Killed some more, take back, ate 'em up. Any time Qwilla *hungry he come kill* Latowni *people. And then he hungry again. Run across mens, womens, child-rings, and kill him, took back ate them again. He got hungry again, came again. Then they came again,* Qwilla *did."*

Qwillas did not care if they were men, women, or children; they killed and ate them. *Qwillas* seemed to have a voracious appetite.

"They ran across Latowni *woman. Take back, for meanness. And, when they get back, he said, 'You stay. Be wife.'"*

Qwillas not only needed food, but they seemed to need sex, too. So they kept one woman from *Latowni* and forced her to stay with them and become their wife.

"And he come again, Qwilla *did. He kill another one, again. They couldn't do nothing with* Qwilla. *He hard kill.*

And Naponohai, *'Where my people? What makes them less and less? What's became them?'"*

Naponohai, one of the makers of the world and a very powerful person in the narratives of my people, noticed there were fewer and fewer people. He wondered where they all were.

"Well, he said, 'I better walk up line here, see. What cause my people go away so many.' He went up. Took dog. Looking around pretty good. He went along. Some one come over hill Qwilla! *And he saw him."*

Naponohai decided to investigate, so he took his dog, which, according to our narratives, is as large as a horse and full of magic, and he began to search. As he searched, he discovered *Qwilla. Naponohai* knew *Qwilla* was the reason for his people being "less and less," and he also knew there might be a fight.

Qwilla, the narrative continues, also had a dog. First, *Qwilla* and *Naponohai* smoked a pipe. *Naponohai's* smoke smelled good to *Qwilla,* just as *Naponohai* wanted. *Qwilla* inhaled the smoke for a long time, then got drunk and fell down. *Naponohai* grabbed *Qwilla,* tied him up and killed him. *Naponohai's* dog attacked the dog of *Qwilla* and defeated him.

Then, Naponohai took *Qwilla's* skin off and put the skin on himself. He needed to disguise himself in order to gain entry into the *chema-ha* at *Latowni,* where other Qwillas had the people captive and were hanging them over the fire from the rafters in order to torture and burn them.

But when *Qwilla* was killed, he had roared, and his sisters and brothers in the ceremonial house at *Latowni* thought they heard him. But the people the *Qwillas* were about to kill convinced the *Qwillas* that it was a different noise than a roar, that somebody had dropped a grinding pestle in the *chema-ha*, which made the earth shake.

When they are preparing to make magic over death, the Ones-of-Power gather something personal from those people they wish to return to life. In this narrative, *Naponohai* found a hair from each of the people the *Qwillas* had killed and eaten, then he went into the sweat house disguised as a *Qwilla*.

Once inside, *Naponohai* plugged up any escape hole. After taking the threatened people safely out, he set the *chema-ha* on fire.

All of the *Qwillas* did not perish. Those surviving were sent out from the land southward and instructed never to return again.

After bathing themselves in Dixie Creek, the people rescued from the *Qwillas* went into the *chema-ha* of *Naponohai* and, knowing they could trust his power, waited for the magic of returning life to occur. The magic happened in the morning, as the people killed and eaten by the *Qwillas* all returned, singing and laughing.

The rock formation of the dead King of the *Qwillas* still stands, not far from Dixie Valley. It is a reminder of this history and also a statement to the giant lizards that they are still not welcome in our homeland. And this is why, the old ones tell us, there are no dinosaurs or alligators in the Pit River Country today.

I was little and hurting, and I wanted to be big and fearless and, like Naponohai, run the bad feelings out of my life, south and forever.

And so because of the accident, I had gone from Dixie Valley with Mom and Dad and the family, to Goose Valley as a ward of the state. One a pleasant memory, the other a frightening venture into uncertainty. For a long time I felt like I had been wounded, and the blood kept running out of me, and the blood was gray.

But Goose Valley was beautiful. It had color, and my blood began to have color, too.

A sweet-gray, mossy rail fence zigzagged along the irrigation ditch near the brown-black, weathered, pine board house. Part of the house was built over the clear flowing water in the ditch to keep that section of the home cool in the summertime. The forest met the meadow here, and both Wonder and Spirit created an understanding between them. Some flowers looked up and over the tallest timothy grass, and hummingbirds and bees were busy flitting and weaving between them. A turquoise dragonfly, appearing much like a long-tailed helicopter, rattled by, hovered, then landed on a tule growing out of the water. Silence.

The blossoms on the apple trees and wild plums hummed constantly as thousands of bees, in an ancient melody, danced a slow ballet, as if underwater, bobbing from blossom to blossom, floating from apple tree to pear tree to plum stand. Such perfect melody in a land of sunshine and color—the music found only in solitude.

My unhappy spirit smiled for the first time. It seemed, after the accident, I had lived my life hurting, afraid to smile. I was afraid simply to *be*, but finally, I was happy—just a little. The peace in the expanse of the valley and silver-blue dancing on the mountains, coupled with the waterfall-roar as the wind rushed through the forest and an occasional blue bird darted under the shade, overwhelmed my pain of aloneness. *Lo'we'chah* watched, circling high above in the powdered turquoise.

Quickly we children melted into the Goose Valley landscape. In the early spring we chased and caught squabs (young ducks and geese) with Jerry Graves over in the tules near Goose Creek. Jerry was a friend of the family who lived only a mile south of us. Some Germans moved onto the property far above Goose Valley, and they often stopped by to visit. The old barn was a wonderful place to evade everybody.

When it was time to get away from the rest of my brothers, I vanished into the old barn. It was warm-smelling, still sweetened by the dried dung of the horses and cattle. A lot of pigeon and owl crap crusted on the rafters, drying in streaks as it dripped down. Mice and snakes lived under the pine-board floor and under the moldy hay, and always lots of dust floated about, made visible by spears of sunshine. For some reason, it seemed easier to breathe in the shadows instead of in the sunshine where the dust curled slowly, like a whole Milky Way.

It was a private wonderland. In the silence that followed long after I had entered the barn, I watched life slowly begin to move again. A lizard resting on an old handle of a pitchfork blinked. A Blue Racer snake slid into safety under a pile of old lumber, stuck its head out, black tongue darting in and out. A part of a harness dangled, like a neglected leather jacket, from a huge nail on a timber. Insects began darting into the sunlight, then disappeared into the shadows. A mother owl over there, babies in the nest, moving fuzzballs of thistledown. And a thousand other eyes that watched me, but that I could not see.

In the tender and beautiful silence, a spider slowly climbed just by my ear. I could hear it "ticking" as it moved gently up the huge center post.

My brothers calling for me, "Babe? B A A A A A A B E ! ? B A A A A A A B a a H !"—broke the law of silence. All the little forms of life instantly hid or simply went silent and motionless. My brothers threw a rock that hit the shingled roof of the barn. The rock skipped for a while, then slowed and began to roll, and finally dropped with a thud into the tall grass growing where the water dripped off the barn onto the loam earth.

Life hesitated. Another rock … then another. Finally, peace.

I remained silent. My brothers forgot about me, and I slipped from my little domain in the barn down the ladder that was nailed directly to two huge beams holding the roof. Making certain nobody could see me, I shadowed along the ditch that meandered north and east through the untended, overgrown apple orchard. Not far from the apple orchard, Daddy once killed a porcupine, on his only visit to Goose Valley. Daddy stayed with us a few days, then he had to leave. Back to the logging camp. That's what he said. And he looked pretty healthy, so I believed him.

We had heard the family of *ha'ya'wa* singing softly. Daddy had a .22 rifle and was using the short version of the bullet, something with just a little more power than a pellet gun at full pump. When Daddy shot the porcupine, I thought it would instantly drop from the tree. It did not.

Daddy did not shoot again, and I was beginning to wonder if he had missed the target completely. Then porkey trembled. Two claws on the limb slipped. Then it began to lose balance and its other claws slipped. It turned slightly over and fell in slow motion like a sack of black sand, straight down, landing on its back. It was like watching a lazy dream of death.

Daddy did not visit us in Goose Valley again. Too drunk and sick, they said. I knew he had a broken heart because I could feel where it was broken. It did not pump good. The blood was good, but it just worked differently than other hearts I had listened to. There was a very large place inside his heart filled with dark pain and yellow turmoil. The pain was laced together like the pieces of a watertight basket, pain wrapped around hurt and fear. That is how much my mother meant to my dad—everything, including all of the children, and including me.

In his ache, he drank wine. It never helped. Whenever I saw

him he was always a little worse than he was the time before. It was his drinking that caused the state to take us away. He could not provide for us, they said. And that was true.

As much as I loved Daddy, I decided I was better off as a worried and lonely puppy of the State of California than I had been living with his drunken uncertainty. In the deep silence of night, I gritted my teeth and vowed to myself that if anything like this ever happened to me, I would be stronger than Daddy. I would not give in to the pain. I would stand straight in the face of fear and I would, like Uncle Ramsey said, "Best it."

In Goose Valley I was usually happy, until I thought about the Old Home Place. It was not far from Goose Valley, just across the rail fence, across the field, through the forest, and five miles on. But between me and home were Lake Britton and the Lake Britton Bridge where Mom and Jerry were killed. Every time I thought about home, I could see that lumber truck racing down one hill to the bridge in order to get enough speed to climb the other side. I saw Daddy running in panic. I saw the old, black car stalled in the road. I saw Mom bouncing Baby Jerry on her lap, singing to him to keep him from crying. I saw fear in her eyes. I saw the wreck, heard the crash, felt the pain. Again and again, I smelled the dust and the blood, then cried. Then I saw the mocking tears of the mean people who came to the grave, and I grew angry. I wished that I was *Qwilla!*

And I remembered Uncle Ramsey's tale about how Silver Fox, creating this world, tired of Old Coyote changing everything, so he caught Old Coyote in a net and beat him to death. He killed him.

One of the old narratives tells us that this is a new world, that "beyond the stars" there is a world where Silver Fox and Old Coyote lived. Silver Fox was inventive and creative. Old Coyote had power, but only the power to change things to his liking. So, no matter what Silver Fox created, Old Coyote changed it.

Silver Fox tired of the changes of Old Coyote, so he abandoned the world beyond the stars and came here, singing earth into existence, because when he arrived, there was only water. He did not tell Old Coyote where he was going, but Old Coyote found out where Silver Fox was and went there with his own magic. He immediately disliked everything Silver Fox created, so he set about changing everything he came across. Silver Fox again tired of the changes of Old Coyote. This time he made a net, caught Old Coyote in it, and while Old Coyote was all tangled up, he took a club and beat Old Coyote to death.

Yes, I could make a net, catch the mean people, and beat them.

That would be good. It would not make me happy, but it would make things better. What *would* make me happy was if Mom and Jerry came home in the morning, like when the magic in the legends works. With Mom home, Daddy would not drink wine at all. I was so mad I wanted to somehow kill that white man who drove the lumber truck into my mother and brother. I felt so small, but so mad.

Often in the soft, green shimmer of my dreams, my baby brother would reach for me. It was frightening, for I was scared of his spirit. He always wanted me to pick him up and take him home. He held his arms up to me then looked and pointed in the direction of home.

Sometimes the only way I knew that I was no longer dreaming was when I realized that I had wet my pants. But my resulting shame usually was overpowered by the thought of lashing out at the ugly world. My jaw muscles ached from gritting my teeth through the constant nightmare, and my body muscles were tired from being tight all night long. I wanted to be Batman or Superman, or the cowboys who wore two guns in the movies. They were always shooting my people, but if I had two guns, I would shoot them back!

Earlier that summer, before the accident, we had heard the sky would fall and that if we were out at night, we could watch it. We all climbed into our ancient vehicle that had been converted into a sort of pickup with a flat bed. Daddy, Mom, and the youngest kids sat in the front. The rest of us were lying on our backs, looking up, witnessing snowflake-like stars streaking across the black sky. A black sky sprinkled with a million shimmering lights, some changing colors like a rainbow, some flashing on and off, some dancing with happiness.

Mom explained that the stars were not falling, but parts of planets were coming close to earth, and they almost always missed, so we didn't have to be frightened. It was a wonder to watch stars streaking across the sky, then disappearing into the vast darkness. It was like watching a dream. How could it happen? How could I see such wonder? But, mostly I wondered, what if one hit our car . . . ?

CHAPTER TWELVE

DREAMING
⚛

1957

It wasn't until many years later—after I had I failed to graduate from high school, then entered the U.S. Marine Corps—that I finally gave up thinking that Mom and Baby Jerry would one day magically return. Up until that time I saw them constantly. *Tosa ow asaq'jam* (dreaming and seeing them) happened day and night. Mom and Jerry seemed to be everywhere.

In the whisper of *ho'm* (wind) and in the rustling in the forest, they were there. In the thickness between the stars sprinkled across the vastness of summer's night sky, they were there. In the silver streaks of *asji* (rain) and in the distant call of the night birds in the hush of *loqme* (silver edge of the world before dawn), they were there.

Often they were in the next room, breathing softly, and sometimes giggling.

They were in the freshness of *getuy* (spring) with its thousand shades of green and yellow flowers. They were in the thick warmth of insect-buzzing summer of ripened melons. They were in the gold- and red-painted leaves of wild apple trees. They were in the diamonds dancing across the frosted snow of winter *chool* (moon). They were in the crisp, soft breeze blowing from the snowy mountain slopes bending the timothy in the field.

They were in the flames of *maliss* (fire) and in the dancing redglow of *loq'mim* (morning sunrise).

They peered through the branches of the pine forest and looked down from the billowing, white *a'u* (clouds) of early summer, floating in soundless beauty across the shining mountains.

They were in the soft V of the fluttering white *la-lax* (snow geese) high overhead, and they were in the soft V laying across the morning waters as *phum* (beaver) moved to a safer place in the lake to rest during the day. They were in all of the beauty of *ti'qa'te* (the world).

But they were more vivid, and accompanied by intense pain, when a huge lumber truck thundered and rattled by, belching smoke and growling like a monster.

CHAPTER THIRTEEN

GLENBURN

1955

I always dreamed that the automobile/lumber truck wreck, killing my mother and baby brother, was only a very long nightmare. I always hoped that she was somewhere bouncing our baby on her knees and singing to him, but that we only did not know where, or were not permitted to know, for now.

I always convinced myself that all of this damage to our lives was only a mistake made by me, that it was the worst of all possible dreams, but that one day I would awaken.

There would be Mom. There would be little Jerry. There would be the old black car. Daddy would be working at the slaughterhouse, telling us the events of his day as he slowly rolled down our dusty lane to home in Glenburn, kids hanging all over the vehicle. Magically we would all be together again. Perhaps that feeling will never expire.

CHAPTER FOURTEEN

POWER IN THE GREAT CANYON

▽

1957

It is one of the customs of my people to seek power in nature. While the human being is complete in many ways, in the understanding of my people, the life spirit is limited, often weak, needing assistance. For this reason we must seek a power or a series of powers outside of ourselves which we identify as "helpers." Helpers can be a trees or animals, rocks or mountains, stars or flowers, frogs or rainbows.

Helpers come to us in our time of need, and they guide our dreams. In our legends we are instructed that people were the last to be created and do not possess the best connection to the life forces that move all about. We need a helper or helpers.

A helper is acquired through a quest, a seeking, a lonesome vigil in a place where natural communication is uninterrupted. The person seeking "petitions" the awesome unknown, comprising nature, to appoint him a helper. If the person is sincere in the quest, nature responds. Sincerity recognized and necessity acknowledged, the person, now authorized, makes the "arrangement" to meet his helper through the completion of this private and often sacrificial ceremony. The helper appears and talks with the person, reassuring him or her that it is only a matter of "calling" its name, or singing a special song the helper provides, and the helper will appear, prepared to be of assistance.

The helper or combination of helpers depends entirely upon the human being and what the human being must accomplish in this time given to each of us. Our tradition suggests that those persons without a helper or helpers may be limited in their life's accomplishments.

An average person needs only a single helper. A Medicine Doctor, a Healer, or a Sucking Doctor, on the other hand, may need several helpers—along with other powers if the helpers are needed for offense. The helpers are the same for the common man as they are for the doctors. The doctor, however, uses his helpers in other ways than for good luck. A doctor sometimes was killed if he had been gifted with power but abused that power— murdering people without reason, casting sickness into other tribes, or causing problems among all the people. So the power and the helper had to be used for good purposes, or they became a danger within the native society that needed to be eliminated.

Our old Uncle Rufus's power lay in a certain huge rock deep in the Great Canyon of the Pit River. The canyon, just west of Fall River Mills, is more than two thousand feet deep, and about three miles long. The Hat Creek Rim is at the northwestern end of the canyon, Fall River Mills at the southeastern.

HOW THIS GREAT CANYON WAS made is told in one of Uncle Ramsey Bone Blake's narratives (he told the narrative when I was very young, before my first grade and before Mom and Baby Jerry were killed. He offered the narrative to me again when I had just finished high school and was preparing to enter the Marine Corps). In 1945 we were all together, one large family. In our de-crepit automobile full of screaming, excited children, we rattled into the driveway in a cloud of exhaust fumes and dust. Uncle Ramsey and Aunt Lorena were home.

Uncle Ramsey was short, thick, and jolly. He was almost pink, while Aunt Lorena was the color of yesterday's coffee. They were a great couple; his eyes twinkled while hers shined like freshly chipped obsidian flakes. Uncle Ramsey was always busy working as a ranch hand or woodcutter, and Aunt Lorena was always puttering around her little home. She was very tidy.

A half-dozen ragged kids and an old black dog poured from our weary vehicle. Confusion reigned supreme. Uncle Ramsey was standing in the door of his comfortable little pine-board home just east of McArthur, California. Aunt Lorena was in her immaculate kitchen, making coffee.

Just as soon as we had poured from the old vehicle in a noisy velocity, silence pervaded the house. Mute, we children were all staring at the candy bowl in the center of the kitchen table.

Usually a crystal bowl rested there containing exotic, tasty objects: oranges, bananas, store-bought candy, chocolate. In these quiet moments a tribe of black, shiny eyes focused on the bowl. We knew that we must wait for Aunt Lorena to say "when" before we could have the contents—which we devoured instantly, like little wolves, the chocolate flavor lasting the longest and best of all.

I don't remember too many worries in those days. I didn't care about anything, except preventing my brothers from having something I couldn't, and when they got something more than I, it didn't matter, really. The most important thing was staying far away from the girls.

When I was around the old people, my thoughts seemed to focus on something—like water shimmering on the hot pavement. It was a wonder, or a miracle. I could not quite understand why, but I was attracted to the storytellers of my tribe. Uncle Ramsey was such a person. As they told narrative after narrative, I listened. I remembered not only what they said, but also the tone of their voices, and the movements of their hands and bodies as they told their stories. My mind registered the long silences between their choppy sentences and the often exaggerated pantomime between their soft words.

They spoke *Iss* (Pit River) and *Aw'te* (Dixie Valley/Hat Creek), as well as crude English. English was strange to all of us. I preferred our languages. And, over time, as the lives of my people moved into the world of the American-English speakers, and our original languages became less and less important, were less and less used, something within the old people hesitated. They saw the changes within our people paralleled by the control of our land by the Americans. And they worried.

I was too young to comprehend the changes the Elders saw so clearly. But somehow it was important to me to know the narratives, to learn from the wise people who seemed to be everywhere. Often they would look at me as I huddled around my father's legs and say, "That child different. He not same as all others."

It may be that I was different from the other kids, who had more important things to do than to listen to the narrators. But it is also true that my native people are unique. I was fascinated by their gestures and antics, their emphases and hesitations, and the long silences between words and sentences. It simply was a part of my destiny to record as much of the "old way" as possible. These stories were recorded in my mind and later, when I entered the university, they would emerge precise, like a nugget, unearthed and washed clean.

Uncle Ramsey was around long before I was born and to me it seemed he would be around forever. Like the mountains and the

rivers and the sky, he was always there. I did not see him as
human; he was something else, much more somehow. All of the
Elders who talked with each other easily were so much more
something!

That day, Uncle Ramsey told of the time when earth was being
created and the mountains and rivers and springs were being
made. *Kwaw*, Silver-Gray Fox, was laboring to make the earth a
dwelling place, and *Ma'ka'ta*, Old Coyote, was there as mischievous as ever.

Uncle said that Silver-Gray Fox made "something" by singing
nothingness into a mist, which took more than a million years.
After another million years of singing, the mist jelled and the texture turned to a type of dough, From the dough, Silver made our
homeland in what is now northeastern California. Then Silver
and Coyote danced upon the new land, stretching it in all directions.

Although the new world had an infinite capacity to provide
gifts, Old Coyote was only blessed with vanity and the power to
change things—even if they were already perfect. He had a lot of
magic power like Silver, but Old Coyote could not create. As a
result, Old Coyote was always jealous. Also, with his abundance
of vanity, Old Coyote always wanted to be the Chief, the Captain, the Leader—and to be insistent. So, as Silver created, along
came Old Coyote to change it.

Silver put his stronghold on the Hat Creek Rim where he
could see for miles in every direction—and where he could watch
Old Coyote better. Below him was a little valley (located where
the Pit River and the Hat Creek surge into each other at present-
day Lake Britton). This was before there was a Great Canyon or
a river, before salmon.

Silver was afraid that if he allowed Old Coyote to name the little valley that Coyote would not give it a proper title. Old Coyote really liked to eat mice. He wanted to call it *Chum-see Akoo* (Mice Valley).

The argument over naming the valley getting nowhere, Silver suggested that they go out and make other mountains and springs, then return to the process of naming the valley. Traveling around, creating (and changing), they eventually returned to the little valley. Old Coyote reasoned with Silver, "You, brother, have named all other places. (Uncle Ramsey giggled gruffly and said, 'He called him *brother.*') It is my turn to name this place right here." But Silver said, "No. You will call it by any name but a real name. Sometimes when you talk you don't make much sense. Let's go and make some more life." And they did.

While creating everything in the new world, and watching Old Coyote very closely, Silver forgot to make a canyon for *It'Ajuma* (Pit River) to drain the upper valleys, where he had made rivers, streams, and springs. Instead, where the Great Canyon should be there was a solid-rock mountain.

Upon returning to the little valley, knowing that he had yet to figure out how to make a canyon from the rock mountain, Silver gave up arguing with Old Coyote over who was going to name the little valley. So, Old Coyote named the little valley *Chum-see Akoo*, and "Mice Valley" it has been ever since. Meanwhile, Silver saw that the river must be made to drain the land so salmon could come to the people so they would have another source of food.

Silver spoke to Big Bass, "You must do this (break the rock mountain into a canyon) so river can run to ocean." Big Bass said okay, "But I am not strong enough to break that mountain."

Silver had to think how Bass could break the mountain. He said that he would give instructions the following morning. Silver thought that Bass could get the power to break the mountain from *Ako-Yet* (Mount Shasta). In the morning Silver said to

Bass, "Go to *Ako-Yet*. To the top. And gather power." Bass did as instructed, gathered power from the top of Mount Shasta, then, getting far back, took a tremendous run at the rock mountain striking it hard with his head. BANG! Again and again he struck. Hitting the solid rock mountain hurt, and Bass grew tired, but Silver again instructed Bass to get more power from the top of the mountain. Meanwhile, Old Coyote was somewhere.

Big Bass returned from the mountaintop and again began plowing into the mountain with his head. Pretty soon the solid mountain gave a little. Ramsey said, "It got weakness." It began to crumble.

Bass rushed back to the top of Mt. Shasta for more energy and, upon returning, attacked the fractured mountain, breaking through, swimming on up into the Fall River Valley, then exiting the valley by the same route he entered, proceeded on up the Pit River, turning and thrashing, making a river bed. Any mountain in the way, BANG! Big Bass made another canyon. And he "went on up."

Silver told Big Bass "You done good." While the Bass and Silver were making the Great Canyon, Old Coyote was up at the hot springs in *At'wam* (Big Valley), cooking quail eggs and looking at his reflection in the water. Old Coyote always thought he was the cutest of all beings. He really liked to look at himself in the placid water.

Upon returning to the Great Canyon with Silver, Old Coyote (thinking that there might be something wrong with the Great Canyon being where a solid mountain had been when he left to go get quail eggs) denied having anything to do with any of it.

And Uncle finished the narrative by saying:

"Looking to rim today, you will see power gone. *Kwaw* and *Ma'ka'ta* ran east up the canyon that was rushing with water.

There were more things to make. Maybe it was then people was made. But that is another story—not for today."

NEAR THE HEAD of Great Canyon, not far from a swirling bend in the river we called Big Eddy, Uncle Rufus had his "power rock." Just after I finished high school, he and I went there one time on a soft summer morning. The sky was white-blue, little gray birds flitted here and there. A robin bounced along the ground, stopped, cocked its head, listening, hopped again. In a fork of a juniper tree a gray squirrel, bushy tail curled over its back proudly, "chugged" at us in a scolding manner for interfering with its breakfast. We walked away from "civilization" down a yellow sand road toward the mouth of the canyon. Grasshoppers fluttered in a variety of directions. Sweet warmth was in the air.

Uncle Rufus was the same age as Daddy, and he was a statesman, always more than polite. They went to Sherman Institute (a government boarding school at Riverside, California), often fleeing from its regimentation. Around the fire in the summer evenings, the men who had fled Sherman long ago laughed loudly about those "old days." Years older now, his hair was turning gray-white and thinning quickly. He was deep-chested, thick-shouldered, and his arms were like oak limbs. And, like most of my people, he was dark-complexioned and stout. His laughter, unexpected, could knock a person off balance twenty feet away.

In silence we walked—just a distant scrunching of the soft sand under our feet. All around us life hummed, soft and friendly. Old Lizard skittered across the road, little puffs of dust rising, then he disappeared, leaving a series of long S's behind its dragging tail.

Three deer bounced just beyond the clearing. We heard them, then saw gray-brown flashes blur between the bushes. Rounding a curve in the road, we heard the crashing of the Pit River below and to our left. We knew we were below Big Eddy and were approaching the mouth of the Great Canyon.

As Uncle and I dropped down the old road into the Great Canyon, something caused me to hesitate. It seemed like a violation to go to Uncle Rufus' rock. I did not have a "helper" or a place of power. But if I did, it would not have been right for other people to walk upon my place or to look at it. I sure wouldn't like it if somebody wandered upon my helper and maybe touched it. A place of power is just too important to each person. I stopped.

Uncle Rufus looked at me with appreciation, then disappeared through the boulders and brush on the left side of the road. He simply vanished.

I waited in the shade above the road, listening to the distant roar of the wind and the river moving through the Great Canyon. I watched buzzards hover far above, as my spirit mingled with the soft peace that was all around. I felt better not knowing exactly which rock was Uncle's power rock, which part of nature was his helper.

After a long while, the bushes moved and Uncle appeared. He seemed the same, making me wonder about this "power." Somehow I thought he would be changed—maybe two of him would appear.

Quietly, we walked homeward. Uncle never invited me to visit his rock again. Somehow there was a deeper respect between me and Uncle. It was as if we had a secret, but he knew that he, alone, really knew the secret. I only got close.

His rock must have been one that was turned over or broken up when Big Bass got the power from Mount Shasta long ago and crumbled the solid rock mountain as it swam on up into the upper valleys. In my imagination, I saw the rocks crumbling and flying. I saw the huge Bass swimming upriver and continuing northeast. It is said that this is why the Fall River and the Pit Rivers twist and turn through the mountain range. Big Bass kept going, it had so much power.

From the mountaintops around Fall River Valley you can see where Big Bass got stuck and whipped and spun and turned and flopped, making the Fall River a variety of oxbows.

I'm very happy I did not go to Uncle's seat of power. In my ignorance I may have touched his rock and altered it for all of time. Uncle has "gone on ahead" now. He has an advantage there in that other dimension. And perhaps he is happy that I do not know his exact rock, because he must watch it carefully.

Sometimes, when evenings were just purple, I didn't quite know why, but I felt sad when thinking of how the Great Canyon was made and how Uncle got a power from the labors of Big Bass and Mt. Shasta long ago. I trembled. I was maturing then, but in the lavender of sunset, I trembled.

CHAPTER FIFTEEN

MAYBE COYOTE MADE GOD

1955

Once, as we were discussing how to find a beginning of all of the universe, I asked one of my Elders how long it took for the earth and the universe to be formulated. He explained that it took a very long time, maybe longer than the mind could imagine. With an old hand, worn by time and burned very dark by the sun, he smoothed out a place on the earth and with a crooked finger wrote "10^{10}" in the dust.

Our Elders seemed so wise and they always gave solid advice. Still I marveled at their knowledge. So simple, so clear. I know that it was because they had no reason to tell anything but the truth that they knew. We were taken away from that knowledge and often our *ah'lo* (spiritual umbilical cord) was stretched to its limit.

It seemed like the more my brothers and I ran away from American society, the deeper we were dragged back into it by the law. We were big enough (I was thirteen) to perform hard labor now, but we were still thought of by the general society as heathens—perhaps savages. Actually, *savage* sounded pretty good compared to other names we had been called.

I never knew the exact reason why we left our last foster home. But now, because of our new Christian foster parents, the Smiths in Oak Run, California, we had another set of laws to obey, the Laws of God. What a magician this God was. He created the universe in six days and rested on the seventh. To live forever we all had to obey His every wish—even savages could get into heaven. But the Americans could not convince me that their laws were valid; neither could God. Someday I would get away from them all.

Before Mom was killed, when we were all home together, we did not "fear" Great Wonder, like the Christians feared their God. Rather, we lived within the spherical laws of Great Wonder, obeying nature.

So my brothers and I from the Pit River mountains had a head-on clash with this God character, particularly the manner he nonchalantly created the heavens and the earth in six days, resting on the seventh. Seven days? Rest! Then we had to ask ourselves exactly who this God made this earth for since it seemed like it was for only one race of people, white man.

Church! Again! So soon?

We lingered on the way to church. Our new foster mother walked quickly down the gravel road under blue skies, clutching her Bible to her heart. She must have been thinking about heaven while casting backward glances at us slowpokes, probably wondering why we were not as excited as she was to get to church on Sunday morning to learn more about heaven and the love of God. I would rather be at the old fishing hole, turning over rocks, looking for something that a trout might think of as tasty. There was an entire trout menu along the edges of Oak Run Creek.

What I was able to learn about God did not seem like love to me. God was a male being, very demanding, very jealous, and, like Coyote and his children in our ancient narratives, He retaliated quickly, using His even quicker judgment. God was precise when it came time to deliver punishment and death to the people who did not believe He lived in heaven and counted every feather that *falleth* from the breast of a sparrow. Fire, according to our narratives, is the Coyote-spirit's best power. Fire seemed to be a favorite power of God, too.

Any menacing, fire-oriented God or Coyote could never convince me that He loved me, or anybody else. Casting people into a fiery hell was not, in my young reasoning, an act of everlasting love. It seemed more like God was committing a crime. But how do you explain to a Christian that the deity they worship resembles a demented criminal?

I did not want to go to the stuffy, old-smelling church. There were only white people in the mountain community of Oak Run, most of who treated us "Indian kids" as some type of curiosity. They also judged our foster parents' ability to bring heathens into the safety of the bosom of God. All of the community knew that our "wild" spirit had to be broken before we would or could accept their form of worship.

The boarding school my father attended was constructed upon the principle "kill the Indian but save the man." Extract the free spirit of the native, radically alter his lifestyle, then inject civilization—in order to make him a better person.

The Christians did not break us, but they taught us how to pretend.

God was easy to fool. We had to pretend only on Sunday; we found out that God only sees what people do on Sunday. We also had to attend meetings at church during the evenings, but they were not of the caliber to frighten us into saying that we loved this authority figure who was about to throw us into hellfire to burn forever. We would fry like bacon, thirsty, wanting water but denied it. That's love?

Mr. Smith had already gone ahead, driving in the old car. It was his duty to be there early, open the church, build a fire, and prepare tables if the worshippers were going to celebrate a communion. This duty circulated among the "faithful" and changed responsible hands each month throughout the year. Our responsibility was to do all of the daily chores before church.

I would rather be feeding the hogs. Or tending the cows that softly chomped fresh clover and little dandelion tops in the sunlight. They twitched their tails at the pesky flies, but nonchalantly went about their business of mowing the grass and churning it into milk, and occasionally having a calf. Nice business.

While at the Smiths', it seemed that I needed a friend, so I caught and tamed a ground squirrel. I often played with Henry. He lived under the refrigerator until he got too big, then we moved him to a pile of old cedar rails weathering under the sun and the rain.

Sometimes I raced through the orchard climbing the apple trees, inspecting for the ripe ones.

Apples. Today was Sunday. Why didn't we run to the orchard, climb the trees, and pick apples, instead of shuffling to church, hoping that something would happen to the preacher so we could go home early.

Applesauce over pancakes. Hot apple pie. Warm apple turnovers. Cold apple strudel with fresh whipped cream. And, in the spring, apple blossoms with bees floating around them in a constant buzz. Sun must be happy during the spring and summer when so much beautiful life abounds. Besides, most of the girls wore shorts then.

Peeling apples was fun. We always tried to make the longest

peel, then throw it over our shoulder while thinking about the name of a girl. If, after flying through the air and flopping on the ground, the peeling formed a "letter" remotely resembling that of the first letter in the girl's name, we were sure there was love involved somewhere. Deep love, everlasting.

I thought about "L" a lot. I volunteered to peel apples thinking that a swirling, cursive "L" would somehow appear in the dust formed by a long peeling, and "L" would smile upon me while we rode the bus to school. She never smiled. But I never stopped peeling apples with expectation.

A black pickup ripped by, dust flying, choking us with the sweet smell of dry earth and the foul odors that came spewing out of the exhaust pipe. I imagined running away with the dust cloud as cover, but we never did, no matter how many pickups dashed past us on that dusty gravel road. Church Road.

From a distance we could hear the people singing and praising the Lord, but I wanted no part of it, even if everybody dressed as best and as clean as they could. A certain look in their eyes frightened me. It seemed to me to lack a truthful connection to the spirit of the earth. Their eyes did not shine like a deer's.

At the edge of the road on the way to church, we lingered, browsing on blackberries that were growing near the little trickling irrigation ditch. Lucky trickle—meandering away from church, unseen in the shadows but silver in the sunlight. Boy! Some of the blackberries were goddamned bitter! Especially the ones that had just a little red to them. Saliva gushed from under my tongue. Green ones made my entire spirit shudder and my teeth "itch."

My heart put on its brakes each time I approached the House of the Lord. All the singing did not make church a pleasant place to me. They read a scripture saying that we, the lambs, were supposed to "make a joyful noise unto the Lord." Well, I agree that it was noise that everybody made, including the weary organ played by a weary person, but I will never be convinced that it was a *joyful* sound.

In contrast, I liked the rooster's crowing, the hog's grunting, the cow's lowing, and the coyote's howling—even wildlife's silence. Silence is more wholesome than all of the church choirs in all the world. The beautiful silence of the woods and of nature was sincere, real, healthy. A hush filled with healing. But this God-being enjoyed volume and racket, because in church the singing was pain mixed with agony and seasoned with uncertainty—not at all like the melody of a meadow lark.

It seemed that nobody knew for "God-sure" if there was a heaven or a hell. Therefore, nobody could tell for certain if they were going to get there, or when. They sure were not in any hurry to join God behind the Pearly Gates. Matter of fact, they hesitated with great vigor. However, the Christians were convinced that all of their neighbors who drank beer and wine, who did not beg forgiveness before the Lord, would go straight to hell to burn in eternal flames. A never-ending cremation, forever thrashing in agony.

Personally, I liked the people headed for eternal damnation much better than those headed for eternal life. There was much more humanity about them. Their eyes smiled on Sunday mornings.

The preachers were different every Sunday. I assumed they came to the church to collect money from the congregation and leave early in the afternoon. Then they would tell another preacher where they could go on Sunday morning to sing, collect the money, then leave. They always departed with a sparkling smile in a new car and a cloud of dust, taking away all that money.

Sundays were the longest, most painful days. Being a labor force for the Smiths, we had many chores, even on the "day of rest." Before daylight the cows had to be milked. I liked being up early because before dawn it was fresh and clean. The air was sweet. Stars were still out. The birds were just "changing shifts," the night birds quieting and the morning birds beginning their songs.

"Early in the day the world smells better. When people start getting up, the world beings to stink," old Grams told me in Likely when I was pretty small. I thought she told me that because she didn't want me to think that her house smelled bad because of its untidiness, so she blamed it on people waking up.

Then the hogs had to be fed, a chore I particularly enjoyed if the hogs had watermelon rinds to eat. They crunched them like horses crunch apples, slobbering a lot and grunting, kind of like they grunted when they were mating. The fragrance of the crushed rind was green-sweet, delicate, and distant, like a thousand fresh orchids. Of course, if everything got slopped up and a hog relieved himself in the trough, it smelled pretty bad—couldn't watch that.

Then, before breakfast and again after nocturnal chores, we had to endure a long Bible reading. Either Mr. or Mrs. Smith would read for what seemed to be half a year. They sounded like they were stuck on one line on a revolving record.

"And Ham began Jepeth, and Jepeth begat Joseph, and Joseph ..." begat somebody else. Finally, after an hour of very flimsy, fine-print pages of "begatting," we discovered that this was a long line of people we never knew and would never meet. It seemed an exercise in futility. But I later realized that this was one way for the Christians to justify the being of God. He gave all of these people directions and destinations. I learned later that God also gave all of the Western Hemisphere to those people's descendants for their personal use. They took possession from the natives beginning in 1492.

Of course, breakfast was cold after all of the begetting and begatting. The pancakes were on the back of the black cast-iron cook stove, drying at the edges. The potatoes, no longer hot, left a fine coat of grease in my mouth. The butter lumped on cool pancakes made another coat in the mouth. I liked the milk. We let it settle overnight then skimmed the cream off the top and made butter. The milk was delicious! If I drank it too fast when it was cold, I got a headache, but it was too good to drink slowly.

The white man's God said to rest on the seventh day because He, too, had to rest on the seventh day, tired from making the firmament. Listening to the Bible and all of the begetting, going to church, mumbling through the singing, sitting there staring out the window or at the spiders crawling across the ceiling, returning "home" to water the garden, then in the evening milking the cows again and feeding the hogs—that all did not seem like "rest" on the seventh day to me.

Labor I could endure, but God I could not. Running through the woods, fishing, swimming, and hunting: that is how to rest on the seventh day! After church and after chores on Sunday we sometimes traveled through the mountains, studying the terrain. Always we planned our escape. Someday we would run and never return. Someday, soon. Maybe this God guy could feed us in the wilderness and guide our path. No, can't count on Him.

I wondered how this God got to be a ruler over the lives of men. They cannot see this God, but they can hear him because he is busy talking with them and answering their prayers. They said he was real, this six-day world-maker. I did not believe them. I knew there was a greater power than God. These people imagined God. They agreed in their pretending, afraid to say they only imagined Him, or they would be ostracized as *atheist*!

The Christians never inquired about the knowledge of Native people. They never cared enough about the "old Indian stories" to consider them seriously. God and the Bible. The Bible and God. Nobody cared about *our* lessons and legends, not even the preachers.

Assuming that their God was the only power in the world that needed to be recognized, spoken with, and acknowledged, not once did the Smiths or any of the other Christians ever wonder what my concept of Great Spirit was. How limited is the Christian consciousness! I thought that they were not free in the spirit of Jesus and God as they claimed, but prisoners of doubt and fear.

I wondered what Christians might think about the narrative told by Lee Bone, a very old person from Dixie Valley, concerning the beginning of this earth, a lesson he told to my people, again and again:

> *There was nothing. Above on the other side of the sky, lots of people.*
>
> *Coyote too rough up there. Silver-Gray Fox don't know how get rid of him. And he, Fox, had big* chema-ha *(sweat lodge). That sweat had big center post.*
>
> *And Fox lift up center post. Fox, he came down through hole and put post down. Coyote don't see. He had cane brought with him.*
>
> *Fox put down upright on water, and he sit on top and singing. With singing made little ground around. When big enough, he sing sweat house.*
>
> *Coyote try find out where Fox at. No one tell. One little*

basket, he said, "Fox down there," to that post. And that's why Coyote he went down.

He come same way Fox did, and he do same thing Fox did.

So he went down and pull it up, the sweat house post, same way.

He went with cane. He come down on chema-ha *and look see Fox in there.*

Fox look see Coyote when he come so he lived with him and so he make big singing all time, make big world, like now.

OUR UNDERSTANDING of this narrative is that there was nothing but water here when *Kwaw* (Silver-Gray Fox) arrived. There is a land beyond the sky where *Kwaw* lived, and *Ma'ka'ta* (Old Coyote) was there, too. *Kwaw* tired of *Ma'ka'ta* and wanted to get away from him, so he went into his *chema-ha*, lifted up the center post, and dropped down through the hole to this world. Just before he left the world beyond the sky, *Kwaw* arranged the dirt around the center post so Old Coyote could not see it had been disturbed. Then he came down a "rope" made from a song.

Kwaw brought a walking cane with him, and in order not to get wet, he balanced the cane on the water and sat on top of it and began singing. He knew if he sang long enough a piece of earth would appear. Some land appeared, and *Kwaw* sang until the land was big enough to walk upon. Then he sang a *chema-ha* into being.

Meanwhile, *Ma'ka'ta* missed *Kwaw* and ran around in the world beyond the sky asking everything where *Kwaw* might be. *Ma'ka'ta* went into *Kwaw's chema-ha*, in an attempt to find some clue to his whereabouts. He spotted a little willow basket sitting on a rafter and threatened the basket with death by cremation if it did not tell him where *Kwaw* was.

All of the beings knew *Ma'ka'ta's* favorite power is fire, and they all feared both the fire and his irresponsible attitude. Little basket, fearing for its life, pointed to the Center Post of *Kwaw's chema-ha*, stating that *Kwaw* went down through the hole.

Ma'ka'ta, with his own magic powers, lifted the center post and dropped down to this world, landing on the *chema-ha* that *Kwaw* had just sung into being. With that *Kwaw* was resigned to the fact that *Ma'ka'ta* was here to stay, so they sang together to make this world as big as it is today.

Another narrative informs us that after a long time upon this earth, *Kwaw* decided to make people out of a service berry bush. He cut and skinned the forks of the bush, and placed them on the roof of his *chema-ha*. Then he sang and thought the right thought. Pretty soon the bush forks began moving; then they were people. They couldn't talk, but they could look around, and they saw all of the world.

Ma'ka'ta was watching *Kwaw* make people. But Old Coyote wanted to make only "womans." He got the service berry forks, skinned them, laid them on the roof of the *chema-ha*. Coyote did not want to make men or children. He wanted to make lots of women just for himself, to satisfy his vanity. He wanted every woman to have his baby. In creating "womans" Coyote did everything just like Fox did, only he had the wrong thought. The service forks turned out to be women, all right, but they were very angry women, and they did not like Coyote. They grabbed clubs and beat him almost to death. Then they returned to their original wood form.

THESE NARRATIVES made me wonder how much Old Coyote

had to do with this life of ours among Christians. Maybe Coyote made God.

Something that the Christians had forgotten to take into consideration is that Mom and Jerry did not go to church. They did not pray to God. They did not intend to go to heaven. They did not even know where it was. They simply were alive, like deer and the wind—until they were killed.

The Christian God would have them in hellfire, burning and sizzling. They'd be thirsty, crying for water. In their agony, God would refuse them drink? It says in their Bible that God would not give them one single drop of water.

God, if you don't give water to my mother and my baby brother, then you are a son-of-a-bitch!

CHAPTER SIXTEEN

ENTERPRISE

1955

I could no longer stay with the Smiths. They delivered me to the court and the judge remanded me to juvenile hall, Ross Cottage in Enterprise, a half mile from the high school.

It was difficult going from confinement at Ross Cottage to school and back to confinement again. Sometimes from solitary confinement to school and back to solitary again if I disobeyed even one of the Cottage rules. It was not good for my spirit, which wilted during that season. My pride was one and one-half inches tall. I measured it all of the time. My value was even smaller. I was, as the history books predicted, becoming a "vanishing Indian." The "I" in my being no longer existed. I had become a zero.

Legally, I was remanded to Ross Cottage because I had fled my foster homes. I had fled because the judge called the other people our "foster parents." But I knew that nobody, nowhere could ever take the place of Mom and Dad.

Mom took good care of all of us kids. Daddy and I hunted, fished, and climbed mountains. We rested in the shade beside the meadow, drinking cold water from the silver-clear stream. We laid on our bellies and watched the movement under the water—

bugs and wigglers, minnows and moss. We walked in the dark, getting used to nature, and ate over open fires cooking those creatures we caught or killed in the wild. We slept under the stars, and walked in the morning while frost was still on the ground. But we made no tracks when we stepped from under the trees to the leaves of the nearby bushes, from the bushes back under the trees. In this way we maneuvered through the forest, never leaving shoe prints anywhere. Nobody could track us. A dog could find us, but a human couldn't.

After the wreck, with my parents and our world gone, my body and my spirit were slammed around quite a bit by the law. And forever after, the law, like God, would be there, all-seeing, constantly judging my every movement.

I decided that foster homes were probably good for some young people, just like the boarding schools my old people talked about were good for some. But those students must not have liked being Native people if they wanted to change into what the white man wanted them to be. They must have had an *Elam'ji* (spirit) that they could peel off whenever they wanted, like they changed Levi's and T-shirts and shoes.

Why can't they turn me loose and let me flee to the mountains?

Daddy showed me how to survive in the land. The mountains took care of him and Uncle Rufus, Andy, and Caboose when they fled Sherman. I could do the same thing. The mountains would take care of me.

I planned to flee. But I was already being jailed for doing nothing. If I actually did something, I might end up in Folsom Prison or on Alcatraz, the island of no hope of escape, killers all around me!

During my junior year at Enterprise I was "rescued" by Gary Curl's family. His parents, West and Lala Curl, agreed to let me live with them in Buckeye, just north of Redding. They were

Native. They did not go to church. They did not believe in God. They were human beings. They knew my people and did many things like my parents. My rebellion quieted. I learned how to pan gold with West. Lala cooked the most wonderful potatoes and eggs with toast for breakfast. Sometimes West would allow Gary to drive the Chevy to school. I thought I was living in luxury. When we arrived at school, I felt like I was stepping out of a limousine in Hollywood, wearing sunglasses, a turtleneck sweater, leather shoes. My life was finally better—except for English.

Out in the hall, whenever the English teacher, Mr. Grossen, said "Darryl" my heart stopped, everything went blank, and a gray film instantly consumed my senses. My tongue turned to stone, and the hair on the neck of my spirit tingled. Because in English I could not place a period in the proper place—and when I finally got it at the end of the sentence, the sentence was wrong. Semicolons and colons were something like Arabic to me, and word order was something that gave my brain whiplash.

In the hall one morning, Mr. Grossen passed by and said, "Hello, Darryl." My heart squeezed in fear so very hard that I thought a hole had popped in the bottom and gray blood squirted out with every heartbeat. Why did a teacher talk to me in the hall? There was something sinister going on. Why was I selected to be sacrificed, and what was I being sacrificed for? Shaking, I entered my English classroom.

I had handed in my paper last Friday, so it could not be that I was late with my assignment. There could be no surprises on the paper itself. My compositions always had more red pencil on them than my own after the teacher got through. I was ready for the F, but I wished that the teacher would make it smaller, or put it on the back instead of on the front, top right. Everybody looked at the grades. I was ashamed. Physically, I ached.

All of the students got their papers back but me. Boy, something must really be wrong this time. What could possibly be happening? "Darryl, see me after class, if you will." Mr. Grossen's soft wish was a command that shook my spirit. Every student knew that something was up, and they too wondered what could possibly be lower than an F. They looked at me with something like pity in their eyes. Already every student knew—that is how fast bad news travels. Everybody knows before the one condemned—the law of the high school jungle.

The bell rang. Like quail, the students exploded into the hallway, scrambling and fluttering. Instantly the classroom was empty—except for me and Mr. Grossen. He dug into his valise and withdrew my paper. It was almost all *red!* I knew it. I was going to get something less than an F, whatever that could be.

Mr. Grossen laid my paper on his desk with a soft slap. Slowly he chewed gum, thinking his words before he said them. My guts were frozen. If somebody had lit a match and stuck me with it, I would not have felt the heat of the flame.

Daddy and I found a coyote once with a steel trap on its front leg and another on its back leg. It had already bled and starved to death and was wilting. It was a horrible and painful thing to see. And that is how I felt at the moment, trapped—one steel trap on my wrist, the other on my ankle. The written word had finally massacred what was left of my self.

"Darryl, there is a nice story here. It is true that your paper needs some work, but the story is very interesting. I like it, and I wish you would make some basic corrections."

Something deep inside my being calmed, but it took a while to register. I heard again, "I like it." He liked it! I could touch the earth again.

As my spirit listened, that white, red-rimmed, splash of trembling fear faded to pink, then it was replaced with something resembling calm. My heart ceased its banging.

"Did you hear what I said, Darryl?"

"Yes, Coach."

"And, don't call me *Coach* anymore, Darryl. Mr. Russell is the coach. I am your English teacher.

"Yes, sir, Mr. Grossen."

After an awkward silence, Mr. Grossen studied my eyes, then he continued.

"This paper needs some work. You need to work on your spelling. Here, take this dictionary. It's easy to carry. Take it with you and correct the words that I have underlined—*and remember how they are spelled, so you won't have to look them up throughout your career.*"

Throughout my career! Nobody ever told me that I was going to live long enough to have a career!

"Also, you have to learn how to complete a sentence. A complete sentence has a subject and a verb, a noun, such as a person, and an action word, as in the sentence 'I jumped.' It can be very long, or it can be very short, but it must have a subject and a verb. You can find this information in Chapter Six of your English Grammar Book. Study Chapter Six."

Sitting on the edge of his desk, he chewed his gum slowly. Another bell rang. Panic! That meant that I was already late for my art class. Mr. Moravec would *look* at me when I tried to sneak in. Sometimes his door was open, and it was easy. But when the door was closed, I feared opening it. He was hardly ever angry at the students for being a little tardy, but he *looked* just the same.

"I have already talked with Mr. Moravec. He knows you may be a little late.

"Rework this paper, making the corrections I suggested. Also, learn how to capitalize and when to capitalize. Always capitalize at the beginning of a sentence and when you are using a proper noun. A proper noun is the name of a person, place, or thing. Don't capitalize *cat* or *horse*, but do capitalize *Enterprise* and *New*

York. You will understand if you study Chapter Five. Chapter Six also deals with run-on sentences, and Chapter Seven deals with gerunds and incomplete thoughts.

"You might look at Chapter Eight because it deals with punctuation. Punctuation makes your words have directions, like signs on the highway. Punctuation guides people through your thoughts, much as streetlights guide people as they drive their cars through town and out on the highway. It shows your readers when to stop, when to turn, when to slow, and when to prepare for the next set of instructions. When you punctuate, pretend you are driving people through Enterprise and Redding, then take them to Shasta Lake for a picnic, and take them safely home. It works.

"Take this paper home. Rework it. Study the chapters I have suggested. Use this dictionary. When you are ready, bring your paper back to me. I really want to read the story. With some corrections, there are many people who would like to read it."

Wow! I hurried to art class. The door was open. I slipped in. Mr. Moravec *smiled a good smile.* I now had my dictionary and my English Grammar book, and I did not put them down through all of the art class. I just waited for the bell to ring. But this time I wanted the bell to ring so the art class would be over and I could begin working on my English paper. A new feeling moved through my body like ink through a blotter. It was a feeling of worth, of importance, of having something of value—a story that Mr. Grossen wanted to know more about, just as soon as I placed the signposts in correct order and worked on my spelling.

I rushed "home," for once welcoming the restrictions at Ross Cottage, and began studying the grammar book. I read my paper over, located every word that was underlined, read their meanings and memorized them. The meanings, in cursive, were etched upon the blackboard of my memory. After dinner I again welcomed the solitude, the isolation of confinement. I could now study without interruption.

I discovered while studying gerunds that "-ing" made words like "cook" come alive. It caused movement. It kneaded the dough and formed the loaves. It lit the flame that made the heat to cause the chemical reaction making the aroma and the flavor and the nourishing texture. "Ing" made everything move instead of sitting still. "Sitting still" even sounded like a motion.

Run-on sentences. Misplaced modifiers. Place a period at the end of a complete thought. Capitalization, punctuation, dangling—dangling what? Dangling ... dangling ... "dangling participle." I found it in *my* text book, page 81.

> Dangling participle. *Grammar.* A participle that lacks clear connection with the word it modifies. In the sentence *Working at my desk, the sudden noise startled me, Working at my desk* is a dangling participle.

LET ME SEE. *Working at my desk.* That made perfect sense to me. *The sudden noise startled me.* That made perfect sense, too. Let me see ... Maybe, *While I was* working at my desk. Yes! That's it! *I* then would be referring to *me* in the second part of the sentence. It was more than perfectly clear; it "stuck." The sudden noise could not startle *my desk.* There had to be something alive that could be startled. And what could be more alive then me?

I had completed only the first page of my six page paper when the metal door of my cell slid open and the "boss" said it was time for breakfast. Breakfast! I still have to sleep!

I hurried to school, carrying my dictionary and grammar book. I took them from class to class. For the first time in my high school experience it did not mater whether or not I saw Barbara or Phyllis. I now had my dictionary and grammar book, and I did not have to wonder or worry if the books liked me. Of course they liked me, or anybody who uses them properly.

I told Mr. Grossen that my paper was not yet reworked. He just said, "Bring it in when you're ready." Bring it in *when I am ready*. Wow! A teacher giving a student the authority to decide the deadline for an assignment!

Rushing back to Ross Cottage after school, I asked if I could retire early. The boss thought that was a great idea. One less thing for him to worry about. The thick door slid heavily shut with a resounding thud, the key turned, the bolt slammed with authority. Wham!

Now I could work on my paper without interruption. Besides, it was not really confinement anymore. I was on the most important journey of my life, upon a vast ocean of words and thoughts and meaning, and I had just stepped from the shore onto the waves.

The last five pages of my story were completed before the boss opened my door for breakfast. I was so happy. I had gone over my paper time and again. It was ready. I was ready.

After English class was over, I laid my paper on Mr. Grossen's desk. I knew he would now have a story to read instead of a lot of errors. That night after lock-down I lay awake thinking over the paper.

It opened with me on the lodge porch of the Silver Pines Boy's Camp, high in the Sierra Nevada mountains, near Clover mountain on Silver Lake. I was hired to work in the cookshack. In front of me was beautiful, clear Silver Lake, filled with trout. It was just past noon. The wind caused the lake to ripple slightly and to sheen to silver, become motionless, then swirl and glisten and sparkle silver again. A canoe softly bumped the dock. The canoe seemed abandoned and wanting attention. It was inviting. My spirit led me to it. We slid out onto the waters, softly thrusting while still balancing to become a part of the motion of the whole world. Silently we swept out into the expanse of the lake, the forest watching, just as the sun was watching. Out there in the beauty and wonder of nature my memory returned to the death of my mother and my baby brother Jerry, long ago.

There to the south in the billowing thunderheads, thrusting up like angry fists demanding revolution, came a changing cloud. It silently, slowly formed a woman. Mom! Soon there was a small thunderhead. It moved up beside Mom and nestled there. I cried. The beauty of nature had somehow transformed into the old longing. The canoe slid across the surface of Silver Lake, coaxed by the breeze. It came to rest in the tules. The clouds changed. I focused my thoughts again and searched, but Mom and Jerry were no longer there. "Just like in my real life," I thought. My spirit shook in hollow aloneness. There in the canoe all alone my spirit and I wept.

JUST BEFORE THE BELL rang the next day, Mr. Grossen asked me to stay after class. I knew he had read the paper because of the way he looked at me, proud or something. At the bell, the room emptied in a flutter.

Mr. Grossen dug into his valise extracting my paper. He laid it on the desk. There was not a red mark—on the front page at least. I trembled, this time in anticipation of praise instead of chastisement. He leafed through the paper. Uh-oh, there were red marks on some of the pages.

With an air of something important being exchanged between two equally interested parties, Mr. Grossen handed me the paper. There was no grade on it. I leafed through it, looking over the errors in the silence of the room. It was softly silent. A bell rang in the distance.

"You have improved this paper immensely. And, it did not take you very long to accomplish it."

"But, Mr. Grossen, there is no grade on it."

"I know. I thought that *we* should make that decision."

We? We make a decision about my grade! This can't possibly be real.

"What do you mean *we* should make the decision, Mr. Grossen?"

"You worked very hard on this paper, and I want to know what grade you think it deserves."

I was frightened and hesitant in that fright. My fingers tingled. I did work hard on the paper. Having started with my usual F, a C would look very good. I was afraid to ask for an A, so I weakly suggested a B. Mr. Grossen took the paper and, in the upper-right hand corner, wrote B in red pencil and circled it.

That night in solitary I had no one with whom to share my happiness, so I shared it with my spirit. My spirit and I leafed through *our* dictionary searching for words and for meanings. We dove into *our* grammar book searching for signs, directions, indicators. We found the "do's" and the "should not's," and we discovered the possibilities and the impossibilities of the English language.

It was academically healthy, a complete exercise. My spirit closed the books with a slap, and we made a pact that we would use this English language to tell stories, to express, to sculpture new thoughts. We began a journey upon the vast horizon of the written word, and we vowed to compose expressions with more music than any melody accomplished before.

The texts at rest, my spirit and I slept and dreamed about the vastness that lay before us. It was the beginning of a walk through the stars with beauty all around and adventure forever needing description.

CHAPTER SEVENTEEN

SMOKER

1956

I was sixteen, a high-school Junior and lonesome. My brothers were somewhere—in other foster homes or wandering the streets, and my sisters, strangers to me all of my life, had almost ceased to exist in my consciousness.

I missed something else. Each school year slipped by with me daydreaming about how I wanted my life to be, and wondering why so many sad things had happened to me already. When I approached the point where I was feeling sorry for myself, almost ready to cry, I thought about all the pain of all the other children of the world. Then I felt better. The wave of emotion building up in my belly and behind my eyes quietly receded. A calm, fragile calm, remained.

Any change of foster homes also meant a change of school, and the few friendships that I managed to make were broken with ragged edges. Stability was not in my corner.

I had gladly departed my last foster home at Oak Run, and so was finally free from that God character looking at me through the clouds knowing what I was thinking and judging me every second. I could not stand living in any foster home atmosphere.

I had fled, was captured, and fled again. Finally, I was ordered by the judge to live in Ross Cottage—jail. Living in jail was much more entertaining than living in fear that God was going to punish me for something I was thinking about. At least I could concentrate on other things now.

As a way of avoiding the continual confinement of being locked in a cell, I tried track and field, because if I joined sports after school, then I wouldn't have to return to Ross Cottage directly. At that time, Enterprise was just a brushy area inhabited mostly by rabbits, and our high school was scraped out of the landscape, piles of dirt still scattered here and there. Putting the shot. High jumping. Pole vaulting. Running, running, running. Taking a shower—and thinking about my typing teacher—almost freedom.

I liked typing because if I pretended that I did not know where to place my hands properly and which key to hit with which finger, the teacher would get behind me and rest her huge breasts on my shoulders, giving me the instructions. And she gave me a lot more than instructions. She gave me chills. She made me tingle. She gave me dreams. She was one of the few women whom I enjoyed touching me—and what a touch.

Mr. Russell was the coach at school. He liked some of us "renegades," not just Indian renegades, but all kinds. Mr. Denny, the principal, didn't have much faith in me. He'd spent too much time chastising me for throwing spit wads across the room, renegade-sized spit wads.

One day, Coach brought out boxing gloves. New. Twelve ounces each. They were beautiful. My dad had taught my brothers and me how to box: how to hold the left up in order not to get hit with the right cross, how to move the head from side to side in order to avoid the jab or an uppercut. How to keep balanced, knees bent, legs apart. "Throw the jab from the shoulder and aim clear through to the back of the head. After the jab, throw the right hand, first under then hook over. Move in an out, back and forth, fluid. Work the body. Work the body! If you break a rib, the hands'll come down. Then hook 'im on the jaw. Keep the elbow up when hooking, gives you leverage. Otherwise it'll be just a slap."

Daddy taught Sonny, my oldest brother, the best. Sonny practiced on me. He used me for a punching bag. I rarely got in a good punch. He usually hit me from every angle. Once we did not have boxing gloves so we made some out of old rags wrapped around our fists. It was like getting hit with a piece of wood! And it was better to get hit straight on because glancing blows would leave wide, flat skin burns across your face. We called the burns "strawberries." Sonny hit me on the ear once, and my ear rang for about ten minutes. We were in the barn boxing. I found the pitch fork and ran him out into the oak wood forest but never caught him. If I did, I would have speared him like a dog salmon.

So I learned boxing the hardest way. Daddy taught Sonny and Sonny used the instruction to advance his scientific knowledge on my skull. Daddy used to protect me sometimes, but he had been gone for a long time now.

Boxing, fighting, conflict also brought other memories to the surface, memories that I really didn't invite. They just appeared—usually after the boxing events were over and I had some moments to think.

MY MIND RACED over the political history of my people. The fistfights among my people are still vivid in my mind. When we lived in Cayton at the Old Home Place, there were always meeting about the government, which typically began in heated discussion between tribal members, then progressed to arguments and ended with fistfights. I could not understand the fighting, but whenever the American government was a topic of discussion, a fight always erupted. I often wondered why my people would argue or fight over what Mom and Dad called "just promises." How could some of my people be "for" the government. Wasn't it the government that tried to kill us all off, not even a hundred years ago? Didn't it take all of our land leaving us renters or wanderers—or both? Didn't it claim that we did not exist because they could not "recognize" our governing body, the Tribal Council?

One meeting was at the church in Hat Creek. I was in the second grade. We had to drive up around Burney Falls, then to the intersection of Highway 299E and 89, then straight on the long stretch toward Hat Creek. The lights on our old car kept going out. Daddy would stop, wiggle some wires, flip the switch a few times, swear about a thousand cuss words, and the lights would come on. Away we went. Lights dimmed out again—old wiring. Knowing the road, Daddy kept going in the early darkness. Whenever a car approached, Daddy stopped, jumped out and begin looking over the car. When the automobile passed, he jumped back in and away we went again.

When we got to the church and the meeting—and the argument—was already in progress. Our side was dead against the American government's promises to pay us for our land. They also promised to give us other programs such as housing. The problem stemmed from the fact that the government did not consult with our people before attempting to close the land deal, they simply assumed that we would take pennies for our ancestral homeland and be satisfied.

The other side was for government programs and promises. The meeting spilled out the front door of the church onto the steps, where the fistfight started.

It was Daddy against his cousins, three of them. I was scared. But Daddy seemed to be doing pretty good—jab followed by the right under, then over. Uppercut, breaking ribs. It was like watching a movie, except Daddy was outnumbered, and he began losing ground. Then my mom handed Baby Jerry to one of the girls. When a man rushed my dad from the side, she stepped in and smacked him on the side of the jaw, knocking him flat on the ground. Surprise. Fight ended. Our side did not win, however; those other Indians continued to ask for money from the government for our homeland.

Long before the church fight there were two sides in the mountains: those wanting to have government programs, and those not wanting anything from the Americans. The families that fought Mom and Dad on the steps of the church still promote Americans, even though the Americans, by their laws and rules, cause us to conduct ourselves as trespassers upon our own ancestral homeland. And it is they and their families who came, mocking, to Mom's funeral.

The divide-and-conquer tactics of the American government have been employed with great success in Indian country. Those who support the American government have always condemned their own people in favor of the strangers. Hard and harsh lines have been drawn between tribes, between families, between brothers and sisters. Hate, having no allegiance, permeates the spirit of the native people and is ever present and prepared to surface at any moment.

Grams was on the opposite "side" of the fistfight from Mom, and Dad, too. She wanted money. She wanted everything, and she did not want to share anything with our family—even Mom, her own daughter. She thought us kids were a nuisance. Often she kicked me when I got near, so I rarely ventured within striking range. When Mom was killed, Grams sold our Old Home Place, gave the money to her white-man husband, and I never saw her again, to my relief.

Our spirits battered but not beaten by the church meeting, we drove home in the dark because there was no way to fix the headlights in the dark. I was still shaking. The stars and the moon were out. It is a good thing that there was a moon to race home. Otherwise, my anger would have exploded. Somehow, within my small being, I hated those "other Indians." I guess it was because, as Mom and Dad said, *they* wanted the Americans to think for them.

Long ago the left and right hooks Dad taught me, and that beautifully timed straight right from Mom, left their marks and concluded the argument over government promises.

NEW BOXING GLOVES! They smelled good. Coach was explaining the rudiments of pugilism while I was staring at the gloves. Coach's words faded away into the summer afternoon glare, and I was not listening to his lecture on boxing's proper use in offense and defense.

"WilsonnnnN!"

Coach was standing in the middle of the room on a huge square pad. He wanted somebody to demonstrate the proper way to punch, hook, uppercut, shift, dodge, duck, bob, weave, jab, right cross. He wanted me to be that somebody—since I was *not* listening to his speech.

Feeling a little silly, I allowed some of the other boys to lace the gloves on my hands while the coach was laced up at the same time. Then it was coach and I in the middle of the room, everybody watching. "Okay, hold your left up like this. Spread your feet like this. Square yourself. Get up on the balls of your feet, on your toes, for quick movement and balance. Lean slightly forward so your punch will have some foundation. When you throw your jab, snap it like this." Whip! Whip! "When you have a solid jab, follow it with a right cross." Swish! "When you have a good shot into the stomach, shuffle forward and twist your torso, giving you the maximum velocity, and hook deep." He doubled his fists hard and smashed his gloves together, Whap! Whap!

"Now, Wilson, throw a jab at my face." I stuck a lazy jab out there. "No! Not like that! Snap it!"

I snapped it to the end of his nose, brought the left in an arch down to his ribs, right hand to the stomach, and uppercut! Coach stood there catching his breath, a dumb look on his face. "Let's try it again!" So, I left-jabbed him, left-hooked him, right to the stomach, but missed the uppercut. That was enough. Coach congratulated me and asked for another volunteer. That uppercut was because coach was talking to my typing teacher.

A big boxing match had been set up for all weights and divisions. We called it the "Smoker" and advertised it all around the Redding/Enterprise area. All I could think about for the next month was the night of the fights. I was matched with a classmate, Dennis Maka. My friend Gary Curl was matched with Doug McDonald, Jimmy Monson with Duane Gerome. Almost all of the "renegades" were on the card. It would be fun. Everybody would be staring at us. Finally, an audience, not just a one-on-one with the principal, Mr. Denny.

As the night of the fight drew nearer, the longing returned. I did not know what it was, but when one of my friends said that my father was going to come to the Smoker, I knew what that longing was about: missing my dad. Now he would be there! Tomorrow night! I hadn't seen him for five years, and he was going to be there! With great new enthusiasm my spirit marched around campus. I saw the fight unfolding, again and again. I saw my daddy cheering, again and again.

The gymnasium was filled beyond capacity. Cool air rushed through the open doors. The crowd rippled, a noisy blur. The ring, brightly lit, sat in the center of the floor. Chairs scattered all around it, and the bleachers were tiered against all of the walls. There was a soft roaring. The sixth bout on the card, I had some time. Leaning against the door leading into the dressing room, I scanned the crowd. No Dad yet. I scanned again. Time for my bout approached, so I reluctantly returned to the locker room, undressed, then put on shorts and sneakers. Coach laced on my gloves then went into the next room to make certain that Dennis was properly prepared. In a moment Coach looked in again. "Let's go!"

I stood in my corner and surveyed the crowd again, hoping to get a glimpse of Dad. Couldn't find him. But still. The bell rang for round one. Dennis and I stood in the center of the ring, Dennis hitting and missing me. Instinct, I guess, moved me. I do not recall striking a blow, but when I looked up at the number of points scored for the round, there was a 10 for me and Dennis had an 8. The next round was much the same, and I gained another 10. I began to wonder what was going on, because I could not remember hitting Dennis.

The bell rang for the last round. I heard a faint "Babe," and I thought it might be Daddy encouraging me. So I performed like Coach wanted, and performed like Daddy wanted. I performed like never before. It went perfectly. Left jab, hook, overhand right, right, right! Then back away, get some room. Dennis was taller than I, and his arms longer. I had to get inside his long arms. Pound, left, right, left, right to the stomach. Missed that uppercut that also I missed Coach with. Jab, jab, right cross. Missed that damned uppercut again! Hook with the left to the head, then to the belly. Kill the body. They said if you kill the body, the head will die. Kill the body! Ring!

The fight was over. I had won. A lot of general cheering—some for me. And booing from the supporters of Dennis. None of that mattered to me. I went into the locker room left the door open and sat down, waiting for Daddy to call my name. I waited. . . .

I heard that Daddy was drunk downtown. After learning that he was so near, yet so very far away, the hollowness in the pit of my stomach returned—that loneliness that belongs to us each, causing our worlds to tremble.

CHAPTER EIGHTEEN

SALILA'TI MI'MU D'ENN'I'GU

1957

My job at Silver Pines Boys Camp was over, and I had traveled to Santa Barbara, California with one of the owners of the camp to work in his lemon orchard for a month. That job over, I had to do something for myself and decided to join the Air Force. I wanted to become a pilot, and I decided that the best way to begin was at the bottom and work my way up the ladder to the top.

Seventeen and sitting in the Armed Forces recruiting office in Santa Barbara, I tired of waiting for the Air Force recruiter to return from lunch, so I joined the U.S. Marine Corps for four years. I would learn of other agonies, soon.

However, my mind looked back on my recent life focusing on the instructions the Elders gave to us concerning how we are supposed to conduct ourselves. A memory of Fall River Mills presented itself. It was a short lecture from Aunt Gladys.

AUTUMN 1953 APPROACHING. My brothers and I were in Fall River Mills, California, on "the hill" at the home of Uncle Rufus (whom we often affectionately called KKKruf) and Aunt Gladys O'Neal near the Full Gospel Indian Church. Time to gather wood for the long winter. Sun deflected softly from the juniper trees and danced off the small ripples of Fall River, meandering forever.

Wa'hach (bread cooked without grease in a skillet) was toasting on Auntie's stove. She always made fresh *wa'hach*, with a special scorched flavor, for us. A pot of beans heated on the stove and *wa'hach* slowly cooking in the pan.

A hungry, hard-working but raggedy crew, Sonny, "Bobo" (our cousin Florentino), Kenny, and I. We did not, and maybe could not, know what made the *wa'hach* so good. We accepted that it would always be there—and always have that unique flavor. We simply failed to understand that it was the thought, the happiness, that Auntie put into the *wa'hach* while kneading the dough that made it taste so wonderful. During that phase of our lives, we could not imagine that one day neither the happiness nor Aunt Gladys would be there.

Our autumn wood-gathering usually began after Aunt Gladys, standing in her front door, commanded us to "Stop playing 'round and start working because winter is comin'!" Sometimes we got sidetracked. Often Uncle Rufus would locate a hidden bottle of red wine. He would drink deeply of it, look around and issue a chest-deep, half-growl about how good it tasted. Aunt Gladys, should she find that bottle, would break it over the nearest rock. Then the walls of her silence would automatically roll up leaving us all on the outside.

But today there were no incidents of wounded bottles. We were cutting a windfall pine on the east side of the Pit River Canyon. We borrowed the neighbor's pickup and rolled onto the bed splittable rounds of pine, about four feet in diameter, that we had sawed perfectly. It was quitting time when the pickup was loaded. Gathering our tools quickly, we headed for home. Yellow dust in the clean air billowed behind us. Great Spirit wrapped around us in a special warmth. The deep blue sky laced with long, flat clouds. No rain today. Not hot and not cold, autumn was just right.

In the early afternoon Aunt Gladys saw us coming, wood and Indians hanging from every side of the old truck. She knew that she would be warm in winter, and that she would have enough wood to cook for any guests that arrived, usually unannounced, hungry, cold, and sometimes just pure lonesome.

Having no mother to love, I loved Aunt Gladys, and once, accidentally, called her "Mom." She clicked her teeth and turned back to the kitchen. I heard Aunt Gladys, at one time, really liked my Dad. So, maybe "Mom" touched an unusual place within her spirit. Today she had ice water for us. After work, it tasted so good. It drove the perfume of the *as-u* (Ponderosa Pine) dust deep within our beings. Good, cold water. Perfect balm for sweating thirst.

From the pickup we rolled the huge rounds of *as-u* into the old woodshed. Parts of the old shed were gray, parts sorrel with black swirling patterns caused by the sun, the weather, and the pitch. Inside it was always dusty, like a barn. First we rolled five rounds in on the left side, rolled them far back and laid them down flat in the swirls of thick dust. They resembled wide but short tables. Then, when we had five of them laying flat in a perfect row, we laid a board upon the first one and rolled a round up the incline and laid it flat upon the first as if we were stacking monster-sized checkers. Somebody's toes or fingers always got pinched, hard. So it went, until the back wall was full, round on top of round on top of round. Then we started on the next row. Even though our toes and fingers hurt.

In the evenings purple-blue moved into the Fall River Valley. Red sun, lazy after working all day long, rested upon the western horizon beyond Six-Mile Hill, then fell sleepily off the western edge of the world. Silver moon made the earth vibrate. Aunt

Gladys did *something* in the kitchen that cannot be described, but it moved the bottom of my stomach and made it lurch around. Made it wonder why Auntie did not call us to eat.

Wa'hach, beans, *spot'le* (fried potatoes), *dose me'suts* (fried venison). Uncle Rufus liked to show off how much cayenne he could eat. He ate and sweated. Then, he sweated and ate. With a critical eye Aunt Gladys watched him and his excesses. If he put too much red pepper on his food, he still had to eat it—and sweat. It was fun. The entire day. And tomorrow, too, would be fun.

Rocking in her chair beside the pot-bellied stove (which heated the entire house), Aunt Gladys embroidered beneath her lamp. She mended, she buttoned, she fixed. Her glasses often wandered down her nose and she had to move them back up again with a deliberate, smooth motion of her hand. Then she continued mending.

Usually, when her mouth was set straight across we knew somebody was going to "get it." Often it was Uncle Rufus for drinking wine, but sometimes it was all of us, for a bunch of reasons.

The atmosphere in the room was so thick that we could not even run and hide. We were corralled by the straight set of her mouth. Uncle Rufus was corralled, too. We knew we could not evade either her chastisement or her instructions that were certain to affect us like orders from an Army general.

After dinner that evening, Auntie rocked and her needle flashed in the light of the lamp. Her mouth was set, absolutely, straight across. Her eyes penetrated the cloth she labored upon. She rocked in the hush for a little while. Then she took a deep breath and rocked far back, laying the cloth and the needle and thread in her lap. She breathed deeply.

"Old Fella [Uncle Rufus], have you been instructing these children properly?"

Awkward silence.

"Old Fella, did you tell them that no matter what the white people say, they must know their own language?"

More silence. Nervous silence.

"Okay, you children, listen. If he won't tell you, them I must. You must know your language first. Yes, we must know the white-man language to survive in *this* world. But we must know our language to survive *forever.*

"It is said, and I believe the old ones when they say it, that when Great Power arrives, when Great Spirit walks down the road out there in the night, he will call your name. When he calls your name, he expects you to answer. But the Spirit cannot understand English or Spanish. He will speak in your language to you. How are you going to know if he says, 'Follow me, I am going home.' Or, if he says, 'Wait here.' Or if he says, 'Feed me, I am hungry and thirsty.'? All these things will not be said in a foreign language. You, he will not say 'Sonny.' You, he will not say 'Babe.' You, he will not say 'BooBoo' or 'Florentino.'"

After the lecture, Aunt Gladys relaxed and picked up her mending, dismissing us with her silence, needle flashing again. Quietly we slipped out to our bedrolls in the woodshed. Her food feeding our bodies and her lecture nourishing our spirits, we curled up under our blankets like a litter of pups. Stars powdered the vastness of time, owl threw its forlorn hoot across the deep thickness of the Fall River Valley, wind moved the juniper and the pine to mingle in the most tender perfume, river crashed through the deep canyon, carrying a message to outer ocean and to the salmon, so they would know that they are welcome if they ever returned. Below the "hill" the little town was silent.

As I lay under my blanket I worried. If *Annikadel* or *Kwaw* (two of the world makers, according to our narratives) walked down this dusty road above Fall River Valley and called my name, would I know it? Neither Grandpa Mose nor Grandpa Adam gave me a real name in either *Iss* or *Aw'te* language, like it was supposed to be—before white people came into our homeland and began changing our way of life. So, if *Annikadel* or *Kwaw* called my name, then I would not be able to recognize it. I could not make one up, that is for sure. They'd know if I did. Tomorrow I must get a na ... m ... e.... Auntie's words thundering within my being, I slept a restless sleep of hard labor.

LOQME (EARLY MORNING), I heard "Babe!" and jumped up peering into the darkness! The hair stood up all over my body, and I trembled. Again I heard "Babe"! But it was only Uncle calling us awake.

"Wash up, time to eat," Uncle called. Oh boy, *wa'hach* folded around *dose me'suts*, cold water. Then we jumped into the old pickup and rattled off to work. Today we were going to cut *qosimlo* (juniper). It was wonderful that Great Power had not called my name last night. Maybe he forgot. Maybe he won't ever remember to call me.

We moved out. Water bottles full. Sandwiches, gas, oil, files, hones, wedges, axes, splitting mauls. Bouncing along, we departed in the early darkness, Aunt Gladys standing in the lighted door, waving to us.

About three hours after lunch, we got thirsty and hungry again. With pitch from the sweet juniper all over us, we rolled into the yard and parked near the old woodshed. Aunt Gladys brought us ice water and, looking at "the old fellow," asked us if we were through for the day. We were. She knew that Uncle Rufus always had a bottle of wine somewhere. We helped him find it after she went into the house. It was like an Easter egg hunt. We looked under the rocks, behind the shed, under the

SALILA'TI MI'MU D'ENN'I'GU · 159

house, deep in the old couch, across the road, everywhere—even up in the forks of the trees.

Uncle could and would work like a mule—until the third or fourth drink from his wine bottle. Then, nothing made any sense to him, especially working. We huddled in the shadows of the wood shed and out of sight of Auntie, ready to run if she caught Uncle drinking. We still had one more day to cut wood.

After dinner we quietly made our way to our bedrolls in the woodshed. Having no rest the night before, I slept soundly.

"Get up! Get ready to live!" Aunt Gladys hollered. We washed our faces at the icy water faucet outside by the front porch, dried on whatever was handy, a rag or an old shirt, then raced into the warmth of the house. The aroma of coffee splashed us full in the face, along with the fragrance of *wa'hach, dose me'suts,* and *spot'le* lightly peppered and heavily salted. It seemed like we ate the same food all the time, but that each meal was more delicious than the last.

When woodcutting was finally through for this year, we had idle moments. They were terrible. I now had time to ponder the words of Aunt Gladys. We were not doing so well at learning our language—everything else just seemed to get in the way, besides, there was nobody to teach it. We just learned a little as the days slipped by.

Today I am fluent in English and use only isolated words or short phrases in my own languages. Therefore, I would not know if Great Spirit walked down the dusty road seeking water or food because I do not know the language that Great Power speaks. And today I tremble because I do not yet have a *real* name. Therefore, I feel that I am essentially disarmed. Naked before all of the communication powers of the universe.

Both Aunt Gladys and Uncle Rufus have "gone on ahead," but

today I still hear her voice. It is clear "Great Spirit will speak in your language to you. What are you going to do if he is thirsty or hungry and asks these things of you?" And I wonder and worry. *Tcu' stuwads'igudzi* (What am I going to do?) when Great Spirit says, *S-d·na, l'am me'suts* (I come. Let me eat deer meat).

Tcu' stuwadsi'igudzi if Great Power says, *Salila'ti Mi'mu d'en-n'i'gu* (I wish you would come home), and I cannot understand Him well enough to follow.

THE MARINE RECRUITER handed me some papers. They were orders to report to the Commanding Officer, Marine Corps Training Center, San Diego, California—Boot Camp. Something got in the way of my language again.

CHAPTER NINETEEN

CHE'WAH'KO

1958

Like laundry, I and hundreds along with me in my Brigade were churned through the boot camp cycle, spewed out into the larger Marine Corps Community in confusion wrapped tightly around fear. My orders were to report to the Commanding Officer, Marine Corps Headquarters of the Pacific, Okinawa. We traveled by ship, and I was seasick every inch of the journey, one that took three whole weeks.

However, in quiet moments, my focus upon my people as I looked east across the Pacific Ocean was vivid. Our concerns were somehow sharpened. Their voices came to me by day and by night, in nightmares and in dreams. I seemed so very far away and so helpless to assist them.

I cannot recall a time when the leaders of my little nations did not lament the destruction of our people and the wildlife, the damage to the landscape and to the world. Through our narratives we are instructed that we are a part of the earth and that we must respect ourselves and the earth with a deep appreciation. We are also instructed that the animals and all other forms of existence (from the stones to the stars) are a delicate part of the mystery of life and that we must revere them.

When the European hordes penetrated our homeland, the Elders watched as the strangers, guns in their hands, continued their "kill mode" which started upon the eastern seaboard three hundred and fifty years prior to their pouring into our tribal areas. Wherever the strangers went they destroyed anything in their path. It seemed as if they were in a hurry to get someplace, but at the same time it appeared that they did not have a destination.

They attacked my people, killing us at random, "harvested" the pelt animals, and massacred the meat animals, and they assaulted the landscape as if it were their personal enemy—polluting the water, destroying the forests, defiling the land. They said the land was "too good for Indians." In a greater sphere of truth, this whole world is too amazingly wonderful for people lacking either humility while standing in the presence of life, or respect while permitted to dwell within nature.

The wise people tell us to dream, that only by dreaming powerful dreams would we ever be able to make the world better—that we could use neither the guns nor the laws of the strangers to make necessary corrections in our lives. Sitting on a hill overlooking Sukiran Bay, thousands of miles from home, worrying about the life forces of nature, I dreamed.

ON A SUMMER AFTERNOON, I traveled with my spirit. We passed through the tall forest of perfumed pines and the shade of oaks and made our way out to a small hill green with new grass and carpeted with pink flowers. Grasshoppers dove and fluttered in different directions. "Earth-huggers" we called the flowers, and smiled. There on that knoll we rested, listening, watching. *Hat'wi'wi* (Hat Creek) whispered below us, silver in the clear light, reflecting a vibrant world. *It'Ajuma* (Pit River) poured toward the sea.

Suspended upon the unseen river of the quiet wind high above were thick billowy clouds. They made living shapes. There, a puppy. Over there a little bear. Then bear changed into an eagle, flying south. Hey! There is a *chema-ha* with smoke coming from the smoke hole.

Sun warmed us as we lay back in the mixture of soft golden grass and pink flowers in the deep green of their leaves. Studying the changing world of summer clouds, we slept. We dreamed:

They came. From *Che'wah'ko* (McGee Peak, a place, the Elders say, where much of the animal life throughout our world was created and dispersed when the world was just being created), they came like a flood. Running and flying, spilling from the mountain north and east across the land. There were huge deer with antlers flashing. Eagles thundered the wind with their wings, and there were badgers and antelope, porcupines and coyotes. Squirrels darted and butterflies danced. *Allis* (salmon) and *salich-law-me* (trout) sparkled in the deep blue. There were grasshoppers and elk, and *wer'ak'mita* (panther/mountain lion) shadowed along the earth, breaking no limb, turning no leaf. Geese and ducks filled the sky, and great blue herons and whistler swans mingled in clouds. There were wood ducks and kingfishers and darting, swirling bats. There were *yas* (weasel) and *kui* (pine martin), and floating alone like a giant brown moth upon the mist of time came *Jema'helo Tiwiji* (captain of the big-eared owls, the one that turns white in the winter).

They came, rattling their antlers and whipping the clouds. They "swam" into time and back onto the land—all of the life that had been offered and taken as food for *Iss/Aw'te*, the Original People. Their spirits revived and their beings renewed, they rushed back to the river, back to the nests of the forests and fields, back to the canyons and mountain peaks. Some of them looked upon me and my spirit, but we were small and in awe, so they moved on to their appointed destinations.

In the distance, and consuming all of space and time, the native music made by rattles and clappers. Then a delicate drum beat and a survival song.

The song seemed old, yet fresh and new. An ancient dialect, not the one my grandmother spoke, nor that of my grandfather. An older voice. A calm, wise voice.

Again we heard the rattling clappers and the little, square drum of my great-grandfather, made from juniper, covered by rawhide from a doe, and bound by sinew. The panorama and the song made our hearts sway.

There, in the heart of the mountains they dwell. It is said by the old ones that the spirits that created the universe still watch from *Che'wah'ko*.

Now, Sister Sun was sleepy. It was *Ma'ka'ta* (Old Coyote), they said, made Sister Sun sleep. *Kwaw* (Silver-Gray Fox) wanted ten suns and ten moons. *Ma'ka'ta* wanted darkness so he could do things and not be found out. There are things *Ma'ka'ta* does not like to do during the day. Man *Ma'ka'ta* spirit chases woman. Woman *Ma'ka'ta* spirit chases man. That is what our Elders always say.

Ma'ka'ta does not remember that most beings see as well at night as they do during the day. Some animals see even better: *dose* (deer), *wer'ak'mita* (panther), *suk'ahow* (owl). When this was explained to him, Old Coyote said, "I knew that all of the time." It is Old Coyote's nature to claim to know everything all of the time.

But *Ma'ka'ta* wanted to hide some things, and darkness was supposed to be his friend.

A changing thought moved across the land, a shadow growing ever darker. Now blood-red rested beneath the orange that filled the areas between the black mountains to the west as sun slipped to the other side of the world. Silver stars danced changing colors in the vastness beyond the rim of the world—a sprinkled rainbow. Moon, lazy, continued its journey around the earth. Forest rustled. Night birds called and Coyote moaned a painful song. Silence.

They came in a never-ending stream, filling the valleys and the rivers and the forests with their voice, their song, their silence. It was beautiful, as were the melody and the drum and the ancient song.

A close rusting made me awaken. My spirit was brushing grass from its being. It whispered, *"Dup'da* (Let's go), We must hurry home. They may be worried." So, in the safety of the thick black evening, guiding ourselves by the stars and the shape of the land and the standing forest of oaks and pines, crushing no flower, bending no grass, we moved, hand in hand, toward our *chema-ha.*

The embers were waiting. When we stirred them, sparks streaked toward the stars like fire raindrops and melted into the shadows of home.

I AWOKE WITH A START. In the distance there was an American flag flying and a bugle ta-taing. I looked across the white caps of the Pacific and thought again about my people and the life on the other side of the world. I hurried to my duty station, the mess hall, counting the days before I touched my homeland again. Only five hundred seventy, and a few hours.

AFTERWORD

❦

Babe, my middle name, is not a nickname. I was named after George Herman Ruth, the famous baseball player nicknamed "Babe." But others of our tribe had nicknames—usually for something they did or did not do. "Caboose," for instance, came into being when my mountain people were fleeing from Sherman Institute at Riverside California and Calvin jumped a train going east to Texas instead of north to our homeland. In Texas he had to grab a train traveling west in order to rendezvous with everybody who fled the institution and intended to survive in the mountains. He arrived back in Riverside (with pure intentions of jumping a north-bound) just in time to be detained by the sheriff and returned to Sherman. He didn't make it home that time. There was a lot of laughter both in the mountains and at Sherman.

So, for my people, the nickname often becomes the identity of a person. One day I picked up the mountain newspaper and read where a person with a long English identity passed on (something like: Alexander Frederick Hawkins, III). I didn't know that person, so I soon forgot about it. Then one of my people came up and showed me the same article in the newspapers asking if I knew that "Buddy" had died. Buddy Hawkins. Nobody ever called him anything but "Buddy."

EMERGING FROM A PEOPLE whose narratives reflect our understanding of the world, the universe and life, and knowing that the first land upon this earth was created exactly where our homeland is today, it is difficult to accept "civilization" as an institution of value. It remains more like an intruder.

But as Grandpa Ramsey Bone Blake would say, "Don't complain, Babe. Don't complain. Just do it better." It is not that I would like to make "civilization" any better, but I would like to see arrogant technology bow before the wonderful and magical powers of life and the universe.

MINE HAS BEEN a long and difficult attempt to adjust to civilization. Civilization encountering wild beauty has always attacked nature as if it were an enemy or a target in a bombing range.

There has been constant aggression by civilization upon the lives of my people and upon our homeland. In fact, at times I feel like a salmon born under the thundering waters of *Jema'helo Ti-wiji* (Burney Falls). Living as a fingerling in the clean water for a while, the little salmon then obeys the great summoning power of the ocean. Trout-sized, it makes its way down the Pit River to the Sacramento, then to the San Francisco Bay. Finally it reaches the salty Pacific Ocean to travel the vastness of the Pacific Rim, and to live and mature for several years in an expanse of endless freedom.

After maturing, obeying the summoning power of its birthplace, it re-enters the San Francisco Bay, along with millions of other salmon, to dart through the brine, seeking fresh water.

Salmon, obeying a Great Law, knows that it must reach *Jema'helo Tiwiji* and participate in the act of spawning, or its species may perish.

Salmon meets the challenge of the surging rivers that fork into the Sacramento, points its nose north, and battles toward its destination, seeking the river remembered from the time when it was still a fingerling and dreaming about the icy, fresh home waters of *Jema'helo Tiwiji*.

However, since the time the salmon entered the Pacific Ocean, a variety of constructions have sprung up along the Sacramento River, causing the fish to detour and slowing its migration. Damaging obstacles are everywhere. Barbed wire dangles in the whip of the river and curls around roots and debris on the river floor. Sportsmen shoot at the salmon with high-caliber rifles. Broken beer bottles, tin cans, discarded automobile bodies, along with other forms of shattered glass and rusted metal, are scattered everywhere. Gasoline, oil and poisons from motor boats, construction sites, and train derailments, lace the water, burning the salmon's gills, eyes, and skin. Poisonous particles enter the salmon's open mouth and lodge in its intestines. Danger lurks in abundance.

When salmon finally gets close to its place of birth, a mountain of cement lies in the way: man-made Shasta Dam, five hundred feet high. The salmon never reaches the Pit River, and *Jema'helo Tiwiji* remains unused for its intention in its original design by Great Wonder.

There, in confusion at the foot of Shasta Dam the salmon circles, circles, circles, perishes. Along with it, an entire way of life erodes. A necessary strand in the web of life is damaged.

Such is "civilization" as it meets nature. Tame it while in the process of destroying it. Destroy it while in the process of taming it.

The salmon has physical barriers and poisons to contend with. My own barriers are political, *profit* being the most damaging of all.

I would like to face the man who was driving the lumber truck that killed my mother and baby brother. It was on the wrong side of the road, engine screaming. The engine had to produce more speed in order to produce money faster. Both the company and the driver needed more profit, quicker.

Soon after Mom and Baby Jerry "went on ahead," Grams sold the Old Home Place. The Bureau of Indian Affairs, whose purpose is to legally sever natives from their homeland, was her willing accomplice. A goat named "Judas" at the slaughterhouse where Daddy worked led the sheep into the pens, then into the abattoir. Judas himself was never harmed while the sheep were all destroyed.

Dad and I brought the old home place alive. We planted a garden and fixed the crumbling house and dilapidated barn. We had great communion with nature, and our family blossomed again. Maybe that is why there is such a lingering pain. For a moment my life was like the soap bubble floating in freedom that we caught, silver with rainbow colors all around it, only to be stabbed by something jagged and sharp. The ache has been long-lasting.

A friend I was talking with one summer morning said: "We come from great people, therefore, we must conduct ourselves accordingly, because we are great people."

Perhaps my children and grandchildren will write greater books than this one, since they each are greater than I. Trusting that it will happen, this volume can be used as a reference since I have attempted to record some of our history. The second step in becoming *it'jati'wa* (a genuine person), may be in loving ourselves and the earth with such determined velocity that we not only learn our languages and begin reconstructing the web of life, but that we sing the beautiful songs of our ancestors, completing the cycle.

For it was a song, according to our narratives, that caused all of the universe to have a beginning. We must seek within ourselves the spiritual terrain from our *watu/ah'lo* (spiritual umbilical cord) to that Great Power, cultivating our personal power and creating wholesomeness with our thoughts and our intentions.

Mankind and technology have placed cement dams across many rivers of the world, causing ecological havoc with disdain. The songs of our ancestors, sung by fresh, new voices, but with the same truthfulness that made the universe whole, can cause those dams to crumble.

It is taught in our lessons and legends, and by our Elders, that The People are responsible for life upon earth. Honoring the lessons then becomes a mandate from Great Power/Great Wonder/Great Spirit that we are bound to obey. All people must obey the Great Law, so the sweetness of life can continue.

GLOSSARY

It seems that each person (myself included) who has attempted to relegate my native languages to spelling in English has had a great deal of difficulty, probably because languages are living, breathing, real, flexible entities, and not something that can be stacked like fire wood.

Because of this problem with translation, there are numerous ways to spell many of the words in the *Iss/Aw'te* language. For political purposes, we are identified as the Pit River Tribe of California. Academics break down the Pit River Tribe into the *Achuma'wi* (Pit River), the *Atsuge'wi* (Hat Creek), and the *Opore'gee* (Dixie Valley). As an example of the difficulty of spelling our languages in English and other foreign symbols, I have discovered fifteen variables for *Achuma'wi* (the latest, Ajummaawi).

In this exercise, I have identified the academic source next to the word or phrase: (P) — Susan Park, (deA) — Jaime deAngulo, (M) — Dr. C. Hart Merriam, and a combination, (M/deA) — Merriam and deAngulo. Many words or phrases come from the works of D.L. Olmstead (U.C. Davis): *A Lexicon of Atsugewi* (1984) and *Achumawi Dictionary* (1966), or have been given directly to me by my people as they offered a narrative or explained how the universe was created (or how the world has come to be such a mess). Their names and identities are given after the word or phrase.

Although they may not be employed throughout this text, I sometimes offer both the *Iss* and the *Aw'te* words: *dose/Ma'ku* for deer. This is to show that there are two distinct languages that are particular to the people that I am from, and that the words are familiar to each tribe and often used interchangeably.

While I must take any blame for any errors within the text or the usage of the words and phrases offered herewith, I also encourage those learned in my languages to offer constructive criticism and to labor to bring a solution to the current volumes of word lists that have been collected by academics but often have nebulous meanings attached to them (if even that). At the moment these lists seem more like a wind-blown hay stack instead of a deliberate academic pursuit.

> (P) — Anthropologist Susan Brandenstein Park, original field notes in collaboration with the people of Goose Valley, Hat Creek, and Dixie Valley, 1930, 1931.

> (deA) — *Indians in Overalls* and other related materials by linguist/author Jaime deAngulo in the Alturas and Likely areas, 1926–1928.

> (M) — Dr. C. Hart Merriam in *Annikadel*, the history of the universe according to the Achumawi people, with Istet Woische, William Hulsey, and Hulsey Bill, at Big Bend, first published in 1928, reprinted 1992, University of Arizona Press.

> Much of the remainder of the words or phrases is from Dr. David L. Olmstead (U.C. Davis), *A Lexicon of Atsugewi* (1984), and his *Achumawi Dictionary* (1966), University of California Press.

Ahew/Ehew, (Aqo)	mountains
Ah'lo	umbilical cord
Ajuma'wi, Achuma'wi	Pit River Tribe, *Iss* (the people)
Ajuma	river
Alu/a'u	clouds
Aqo'salektawi, Qosalektawi	the people who dwell near the mountain
Allis/Anni	salmon (general)
Annikadel (M)	wisest man
Ap'as/sta'liwa	edible roots (harvested in early spring)
Aponaha	one of the world makers; also, *Aponikahai* from Lela Grant Rhoades and John LaMarr
Asji	rain
As-u	Ponderosa Pine
Atsuge'wi	Hat Creek Tribe, *Aw'te* (the people)
Atun	younger brother
At'wam/Akwi (Akoo/aqo)	valley
Aw/te	Hat Creek People
Bo-ma-Rhee	Fall River Valley
(P) Chema-ha	(ceremonial roundhouse /dwelling)
Che'wah'ko (M)	McGee Peak/Thousand Lakes Valley area
Chickasaw	(eastern tribe)
Choctaw	(eastern tribe)
Chool/Jul	Sun Woman and Moon Man, each is identified as Chool or Jul
Chum-see Akoo	Mice Valley (where Hat Creek and Pit River join) from Ramsey Bone Blake

Cla'cla	variable of *Kla'kla*
Dose/Ma'ku	deer
Dose mesuts	deer meat (venison)
Dup'da	(this person is leaving; let's go)
Eju'juji/Papuji	springs (fresh water)
Elam'ji/Waski	Spirit (soul)
Ene'he'lawa	falls in Great Canyon (*Inala-haliva*)
Et'wi/la'we'ja	Eagle (M: *Wa'law'chah*, Cloud Maiden / *Low'we'chah*, Eagle Woman)
Getuy	spring season
Hamma'wi	Pit River community area including Likely, California
Hat'wi'wi	Hat Creek
Ha'yanna	skunk
Ha'ya'wa	porcupine
Ho'm	wind
How'ta/Asjomi	rattlesnake
Inalah-Haliva	falls in Great Canyon
Iss	the people (*Achomawi*)
It'Ajuma	Pit River (Big River)
It'jati'wa (deA)	genuine man
Jamat	fawn
Jamol	coyote
Jema'helo Tiwiji	(captain of the white owls) Burney Falls appearance during freezing winter months—from Ramsey Bone Blake
Jul/Chool	Sun Woman or Moon Man
Kla'kla/Cla'cla	moccasin
Kosalekt'wi	see: Aqo'selekta'wi
Kui	pine martin
Kwaw	Silver-Gray Fox

	(one of the world makers)
La-lax	snow goose
L'am	eat
Latowni (P)	ceremonial roundhouse where Pittville, California, now is currently established
L'hepta	let's go; this person is leaving
Loqme	silver of first light; approaching morning; in the morning
Lo'we'chah (M)	Eagle Woman, transformed from Cloud Maiden
Ma'ka'ta/Jamol	coyote
Maliss	fire
Merikans	Americans
Me'suts	meat
MisMisa	power inside Mt. Shasta balancing the universe from Craven Gibson, *Atwam*
"Merkans"	derogatory word for "Americans" used by some Iss/Aw'te
Me'rek'meta/we'rek'meta, Ori'aswi	mountain lion/wildcat
Naponohai (P) (Also: Napona'ha)	one of the world makers
Ni'lladu'wi	wandering person (rootless, white or black person)
Nitsnika (P)	lizard whose roundhouse was burned by Wu'ches'erik (Loon Woman / Coyote's Daughter)
Opore'gee	dialect of Hat Creek employed by people living in Dixie Valley.
Oriaswi	wildcat
Papuji/ejujuji	fresh water springs

Piriki/Wah'jo	grizzley bear
Phum	beaver
Qosimlo	juniper
Qwillas (P)	dinosaur lizards who attacked the people at Latowni
S-d·na (deA)	"I come"
Salich-law-me (P)	trout
Salila'ti Mi'mu d'enn'i'gu (deA)	"I wish you would come home"
Silla	Canadian Goose
Spaheli	potatoes
Suk'ahow	owl
Tcu'stuwads'igudzi (deA)	"What am I going to do?"
Ticado Hedache (M)	World's Heart, one of the world makers
Tila-tosi	insane or drunk
Ti'qa'te	the world
Tolol	all, everything everywhere
Tosaq-jami ajog jehe (M/deA)	"The design on the cup and the basket is beautiful"
Tuwut'lamit Wusche	Infernal Caverns, near Likely, California
Wa'hach/wahaj	bread slowly cooked in skillet without grease, thick like chewy pizza crust
Wa-low-chah (M)	Cloud Maiden
Wa'tu	umbilical cord root
Wayaki/Semu	wolf
Wer'ak'meta/oriaswi	panther/mountain lion
Wu'ches'erik (P)	Loon Woman / Coyote's Daughter
Yaj	weasel
Ya'neena At'wam / Chumsi Akoo (Akwu)	Mice Valley, at the confluence of Hat Creek and Pit River—from Ramsey Bone Blake

ABOUT THE AUTHOR

Born in 1939 at the confluence of the Fall River and the Pit River in northeastern California, Darryl Babe Wilson was a member of the Achumawe and Atsugewi tribes. He received a B.A. from the University of California at Davis and earned a Ph.D. in 1997 from the University of Arizona at Tucson. The father of seven sons, Wilson was known throughout California as a storyteller and advocate for cultural revival. His previous works include *Surviving in Two Worlds* (University Press of Texas), which he coauthored with Lois Hogle.

Courtesy of Dugan Aguilar

HEYDAY
into California

About Heyday

Heyday is an independent, nonprofit publisher and unique cultural institution. We promote widespread awareness and celebration of California's many cultures, landscapes, and boundary-breaking ideas. Through our well-crafted books, public events, and innovative outreach programs we are building a vibrant community of readers, writers, and thinkers.

Thank You

It takes the collective effort of many to create a thriving literary culture. We are thankful to all the thoughtful people we have the privilege to engage with. Cheers to our writers, artists, editors, storytellers, designers, printers, bookstores, critics, cultural organizations, readers, and book lovers everywhere!

We are especially grateful for the generous funding we've received for our publications and programs during the past year from foundations and hundreds of individual donors. Major supporters include:

Anonymous (3); Advocates for Indigenous California Language Survival; Arkay Foundation; Richard and Rickie Ann Baum; Randy Bayard; Jean and Fred Berensmeier; Joan Berman and Philip Gerstner; Nancy Bertelsen; Barbara Boucke; Beatrice Bowles; Jamie and Philip Bowles; California Historical Society; California Humanities; California Rice Commission; California Wildlife Foundation/California Oaks; The Campbell Foundation; Candelaria Fund; John and Nancy Cassidy; Graham Chisholm; The Christensen Fund; Jon Christensen; Lawrence Crooks; Nik Dehejia; Topher Delaney; Chris Desser and Kirk Marckwald; Frances Dinkelspiel and Gary Wayne; The Roy & Patricia Disney Family Foundation; Tim Disney; The Durfee Foundation; Endangered Habitats

League; Marilee Enge and George Frost; Richard and Gretchen Evans; John Gage and Linda Schacht; Wallace Alexander Gerbode Foundation; Patrick Golden; Walter & Elise Haas Fund; Penelope Hlavac; Charles and Sandra Hobson; Nettie Hoge; Donna Ewald Huggins; Inlandia Institute; JiJi Foundation; Claudia Jurmain; Kalliopeia Foundation; Marty Krasney; Abigail Kreiss; Guy Lampard and Suzanne Badenhoop; David Loeb; Judith Lowry-Croul and Brad Croul; Sam and Alfreda Maloof Foundation for Arts & Crafts; Manzanar History Association; Nion McEvoy and Leslie Berriman, in honor of Malcolm Margolin; Heather McFarlin; The Giles W. and Elise G. Mead Foundation; Richard Nagler; National Wildlife Federation; The Nature Conservancy; Steven Nightingale and Lucy Blake; Northern California Water Association; Julie and Will Parish; Ronald Parker; The Ralph M. Parsons Foundation; Jeannene Przyblyski; James and Caren Quay; Susan Raynes; Alan Rosenus; The San Francisco Foundation; San Francisco Heritage; San Manuel Band of Mission Indians; Greg Sarris; Ron Shoop; Stanley Smith Horticultural Trust; William Somerville; Liz Sutherland; Roselyne Swig; Thendara Foundation; Jerry Tone and Martha Wyckoff; Sonia Torres; Michael and Shirley Traynor; Lisa Van Cleef and Mark Gunson; Stevens Van Strum; Marion Weber; Sylvia Wen and Mathew London; Valerie Whitworth and Michael Barbour; Cole Wilbur; Peter Wiley and Valerie Barth; and Yocha Dehe Wintun Nation.

Board of Directors
Richard D. Baum (Cochair), Steve Costa, Nettie Hoge (Cochair), Marty Krasney, Guy Lampard (Chairman Emeritus), Ralph Lewin, Praveen Madan, Michael McCone (Chairman Emeritus), Alexandra Rome, Sherrie Smith-Ferri, Sonia Torres, Michael Traynor, Lisa Van Cleef, and Lucinda Watson.

Getting Involved
To learn more about our publications, events and other ways you can participate, please visit www.heydaybooks.com.